WILD IRIS (BLUE FLAG), FOUND IN BOG AREAS OF STATE PARKS ON MINNESOTA'S NORTH SHORE

Prepared by the Special Publications Division
National Geographic Society, Washington, D.C.

AMERICA'S

OUTDOOR WONDERS
State Parks and Sanctuaries

ANNIE GRIFFITHS

America's Outdoor Wonders: *State Parks and Sanctuaries*

Contributing Authors: THOMAS B. ALLEN, SEYMOUR L. FISHBEIN, DIXIE FRANKLIN, JANE R. McCAULEY, MICHAEL W. ROBBINS

Contributing Photographers: JAMES P. BLAIR, RAYMOND GEHMAN, ANNIE GRIFFITHS, DAVID ALAN HARVEY, THOMAS NEBBIA

Published by THE NATIONAL GEOGRAPHIC SOCIETY
GILBERT M. GROSVENOR, *President and Chairman of the Board*
MELVIN M. PAYNE, *Chairman Emeritus*
OWEN R. ANDERSON, *Executive Vice President*
ROBERT L. BREEDEN, *Senior Vice President, Publications and Educational Media*

Prepared by THE SPECIAL PUBLICATIONS DIVISION
DONALD J. CRUMP, *Director*
PHILIP B. SILCOTT, *Associate Director*
BONNIE S. LAWRENCE, *Assistant Director*

Staff for this Book
MARY ANN HARRELL, *Managing Editor*
CHARLES M. KOGOD, *Illustrations Editor*
MARIANNE R. KOSZORUS, *Art Director*
JODY BOLT, *Consulting Art Director*
SALLIE M. GREENWOOD, *Project Planner*
GAIL N. HAWKINS, MONIQUE F. EINHORN, *Senior Researchers*

SEYMOUR L. FISHBEIN, CHARLES M. KOGOD, JANE R. McCAULEY, H. ROBERT MORRISON, SUZANNE VENINO, *Picture Legend Writers*

PETER J. BALCH, KEVIN Q. STUEBE, *Map Research and Production*

SHARON KOCSIS BERRY, STUART E. PFITZINGER, *Illustrations Assistants*

Engraving, Printing, and Product Manufacture
ROBERT W. MESSER, *Manager*
GEORGE V. WHITE, *Assistant Manager*
DAVID V. SHOWERS, *Production Manager*
GEORGE J. ZELLER, JR., *Production Project Manager*

GREGORY STORER, *Senior Assistant Project Manager*
MARK R. DUNLEVY, *Assistant Production Manager*
TIMOTHY H. EWING, *Production Assistant*
CAROL ROCHELEAU CURTIS, MARY ELIZABETH ELLISON, ROSAMUND GARNER, BRIDGET A. JOHNSON, ARTEMIS S. LAMPATHAKIS, SANDRA F. LOTTERMAN, ELIZA C. MORTON, CLEO E. PETROFF, VIRGINIA A. WILLIAMS, *Staff Assistants*

ELISABETH MacRAE-BOBYNSKYJ, *Indexer*

NATIONAL GEOGRAPHIC PHOTOGRAPHER JAMES P. BLAIR

N atural beauty comes first when Americans say why they *Foreword* choose a place for outdoor recreation. That's one of the things we found out in a recent survey sponsored by the National Geographic Society. I wasn't surprised. I live for that myself—to escape to an open, beautiful, familiar place. I can think clearly, recharge the creative batteries, and revive my spirit.

What astonishes me in this regard is more complex. Recently, as a member of the President's Commission on Americans Outdoors, I criss-crossed this country for a year and a half listening to fellow citizens, exchanging ideas, discussing what people prefer to do at different ages, in different places or seasons; where they go; what they enjoy most. What amazes and heartens me is the depth of understanding Americans show on issues of public policy. In particular, they—no, make that we—we appreciate and comprehend the cost of our parks and wildlife refuges, our beaches and forests. Generally, we agree that tax money must help preserve wildlife, and that user fees must help support swimming facilities and hiking trails and snowmobile trails and campgrounds.

We know that outdoor beauty is a national treasure. But did you know that *state* recreation lands alone add up to, roughly, a total of 96,000 square miles? That's about the area of Oregon, and larger than Great Britain. And did you know that state spending for these lands, adjusted for inflation, dropped 17 percent in 1980-83? Yet we want our parks maintained: I'll never forget a big-city resident complaining of a park where "some of the same chicken bones have been there for years."

Volunteers do a fine job of keeping up recreation areas in many places. Volunteers are a great natural resource across America that must be harnessed—they're dynamite people. Some states are reviving the concept of the Civilian Conservation Corps that built up so many parks, state and federal, in the 1930s. Volunteerism, grass roots participation, public and private partnerships, profits and non-profits must band together, particularly in our urban environment. We desperately need innovative programs such as greenways—connective land between urban centers—for biking and hiking. I wish you could hear the Mayor of Trenton on the value of a park with a basketball court: "You don't throw stones when you've got balls to throw around." Or a 13-year-old girl in Minneapolis on the joys of summer fishing trips with her family: "Many memories have been made on those Sundays."

This book brings you vistas of natural beauty, and introduces you to people having a whale of a good time in them. I hope it prompts *you* to look closely at the needs of your own community, and to be sensitive to lovely areas close to home. Local action, led by a few concerned citizens, has given us some of the splendid sanctuaries you'll see in this book. I hope you'll remember the words of one of these leaders, the late Judge C. R. Magney: "State parks are every man's country estate." Today, I'm sure, he would say: "the country estate of every individual—of our children, and our children's children." Welcome, now, to that estate.

The future of your estate is in your hands, for you, as citizen conservationists, to safeguard.

Gilbert M. Grosvenor
President and Chairman of the Board,
National Geographic Society

Wallowa Lake State Park links civilization with wilderness in the area of eastern Oregon locally called "the Switzerland of America." At left, summer anglers hoping for rainbow trout utilize a raft also used for picnic meals afloat.

DAVID ALAN HARVEY

SUMMER IN SOUTHERN

PARKLANDS

By Jane R. McCauley
Photographs by Raymond Gehman

11

T he road winds forlornly under the low-slung branches of oaks filigreed in Spanish moss. Then a footpath stretches across open country to a broad horizon of powdery sand. Atop this white ridge, a few sedges and grasses bow and whisper; beyond it, untrimmed and dense, they slope to the edge of a lake's calm waters. Off to one side, a plump tree has given itself over to the mosses that net its shiny leaves.

There's movement along this ridge at almost any hour, most obviously at dusk. That's when the white-tailed deer come out to forage, armadillos scurry about, and the bobwhites whistle to one another. As twilight's glow yields to moonlight, a bit of breeze kicks up, rustling the leaves of the tall oaks. Their shadowy silhouettes pattern the rich earth below, while the hooting of the barred owls rises mournfully out of the treetops.

Walking along any of the roads that lace Lake Kissimmee State Park can create such a sense of remoteness—hard to believe, perhaps, about an hour's drive from populous Orlando. In great numbers sightseers come to savor the city's flashy attractions—Sea World, Mystery Fun House, even a Tupperware museum. Not far away sprawls Disney World, with 23 million expected in 1987. But beyond it, skyscrapers yield to marshy fields, roads narrow and quieten, and tucked past a bend in one backroad lies Lake Kissimmee Park. So off the beaten path, in fact, that one frustrated traveler exclaimed: "People have heard of that park, but it is the only one in the state they can't direct you to."

Lake Kissimmee preserves the flavor of the country that Marjorie Kinnan Rawlings made famous in such classics as *The Yearling* and *Cross Creek*. She recognized the "tumult of life" only visible after many walks past pine trees and gallberry bushes, wild plums and magnolias. She found fulfillment of deep needs in the blandness of the season, the songs of the birds, and the rains sweeping through the hardwoods. She saw the palms as aeolian harps, knew softness in the brush of the pine needles. In my week at Lake Kissimmee, I found those same enchantments as well as some magic of my own.

The Florida backcountry of old was a stirring beginning for a trip that took me across the South to six state parks. Summer's heat and the whizzing of the katydids followed me all the way. Most parks lured me for their scenic vistas; one, in Kentucky, for its commemoration of the horse.

But it was at Lake Kissimmee that I encountered an unrivaled variety of landscapes and moods. In its 5,030 acres, woodlands bathed in heady scent alternate hardy palms with deep green pines. Wedged between, hammocks—areas of rich humus soil—hold stands of

Lake Kissimmee State Park

FLORIDA: NEAR ORLANDO
5,030 ACRES

Summer's showcase of water lilies begins on Tiger Cove. Area fishermen favor its marshy backwaters for the largemouth bass hiding under the pads.
PRECEDING PAGES: *Dawn sky flames above a lone pine rising in lifting mist along a stretch of the park's 2,000 acres of virtually undisturbed prairie.*

ancient live oaks. Veiled against the hot sun by their delicate mosses, the oaks encourage a mystical atmosphere, as do the overwhelmingly still marshes and swamps that wreathe the park. Rawlings thought the hammocks shared with marshes and swamps "the great mystery of Florida." To her the woodlands seemed more open, and therefore more hospitable.

Such contrast is best experienced in the park's backwater stretches, off limits by car and too big to cover on foot within a week. Thanks to ranger George Aycrigg, I got to glimpse nearly all of them. In his truck, he took me and photographer Raymond Gehman along the dusty service roads that slice through two thousand acres of unmarred prairie. Not prairie as I had thought of it, but an expanse of wiry grasses shimmering in endless waves right to the shores of the park's bordering lakes: 35,000-acre Lake Kissimmee to the east; Lake Tiger to the south; Lake Rosalie to the west. Numerous creeks and streams gather these lakes together at the headwaters of the vast Everglades. Early morning brings out the mists, rising over the creamy lilies and water hyacinths. Cattle stand belly deep, with herons and cranes clattering overhead.

Wave action shaped this flat country millions of years ago, and even now water continues to alter it. I encountered a startling instance of this by Lake Rosalie. Waiting there for George and Raymond, I took in the unconstrained beauty of the grasses swirling and tossing in unison with the maples, ashes, and tupelos. I heard the wind, the silence afterward. I looked up at vultures wheeling in the flawless sky, and downward, at fine, taupe soil as cracked and crinkly as parchment. I stooped and poked a finger into the ground, and invisible lukewarm water trickled gently over my skin. The unpredictability of this earth made me wary.

Some of the drainage from Lake Rosalie, George explained later, is controlled by a canal built by ranchers in 1948. But since the state acquired the land in 1970, the state has been working to restore natural conditions. Says George, "I've seen this land under two feet of water in the rainy season."

Piney woods meshed with prairie when we reached Buster Island. "Island" in this case simply means elevated ground, and "Buster" recalls a Seminole of the late 19th century, known as Billy Buster. For years he roamed these lands alone, supposedly banished from his tribe for killing his brother. The pines attract eagles, and I recognized the telltale cluster of rags and sticks—a nest—in one spindly tree. In the pitch black of night this countryside often comes alive with the screams of bobcats that lurk in its deepest recesses. I heard only a rufous-sided towhee singing *drink-your-tea-ee.*

In a stroll along the nature trail, the slight shifting of palmetto fans recalled for me an old-timer's question: "Have you seen one bend before the wind, lay all its fans out straight, and just give so's the wind can't find nothin' to take hold of?" George stopped to pick up a baby armadillo lying in the path. "I'm supposed to get rid of it," he said sheepishly. Armadillos are newcomers, and Florida parks, as he explained, seek to maintain plants and animals as they appeared when the Spanish first stepped ashore.

Policy makes an exception, however, for the long-horned Andalusian cattle that have shaped much of this region's history. The

Spaniards introduced them in the early 1500s, and Lake Kissimmee marks the center of the industry that later grew up around them.

Outside the park's maintenance shed, I ran into ranger Clint McKnight, who told me about those years and the role of blacks in the ranching business. "You ought to see those Yankee visitors," he laughed, "when I tell them I'm a Florida Cracker."

Clint was referring to a popular feature of the park's re-created cow camp. Rangers in costume tell of "cow-hunting" days against a backdrop of prairie and a herd of gaunt longhorns in a nearby corral. One Saturday morning, beneath an enormous oak, I heard Jim Poole drawling a tale of suffering with swamp fever, driving 500 head of scrub cattle, and surviving on swamp cabbage and wild hogs. Jim cut a tidier figure than the Cracker cow hunters that the artist Frederic Remington saw in 1895: "wild looking individuals whose hanging hair, drooping hats, and generally bedraggled appearance would remind you at once of the Spanish moss which hangs so quietly and helplessly to the limbs of the oaks out in the swamps."

Of the 40,000 or so who make their way to the park each year, about 5,000 are drawn by the cow camp. Locals come for the bass fishing, and church groups often gather at the picnic tables. But it was wandering through the park's unusual landscapes that gave me the most satisfaction. Though I was often alone, I was never lonely. As Marjorie Kinnan Rawlings noted, there was always a "stirring in the tree-tops, as though on the stillest days the breathing of the earth is yet audible." I also heard the earth's pulsing in the rippling of the prairies, the whir of birds taking wing, and the slight commotion of the mirrory waters at dawn and dusk.

Brazos Bend State Park

And I encountered all that again at Brazos Bend State Park, 30 miles southwest of Houston, Texas. Like Kissimmee, it is best appreciated on foot. Here the 15 miles of trail take you close to pond sliders (small turtles) basking on logs, herons stabbing for crayfish, even alligators decorated in duckweed. And in Texas parks, armadillos—a native species—are protected. Elaine Kenny, a Floridian turned Texas (park) ranger, appraises the park this way: "Though I was raised close to the Everglades, I haven't been anywhere else like this where I can wander a boardwalk right next to a heron rookery. You can't be here very long and not fall in love with it."

It was an early June evening when I began sampling the pleasures of this 4,897-acre sanctuary. Brazos Bend lures naturalists in droves, and I was in the hands of three experts: environmental analyst Bob Honig, a keen bird-watcher; botanist Doug Williams, from the Houston Arboretum; and forester Theresa Callery. Birders favor winter here, when migratory waterfowl overrun the park's five lakeshores. But we spotted quite an assortment: black-bellied whistling-ducks, red-winged blackbirds, a yellow-crowned night-heron, and northern parula warblers among them. And at Brazos Bend, the barred owls like to perch on the stop signs, as though to direct traffic. Ah well, night life in the marshes!

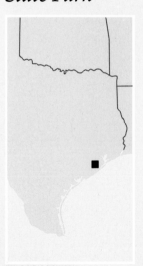

TEXAS: NEAR HOUSTON
4,897 ACRES

Shortly after sunrise, we were plodding through the muddy, three-mile Brazos River Trail, guarded by dense oaks and heady pecans. Droplets of dew spilled from the blossoms of trumpet vines latching one branch to another. A Carolina wren released her song, cheering us on through the serene woodland. The idyllic mood broke only when Doug happened to mention the possibility of water moccasins underfoot, and the reality of poison ivy vines in shrublike masses overhead.

Before the blistering sun neared zenith, we headed over to the open stretches around Forty Acre Lake. Baby coots waddled by, purple gallinules in yellow anklets swam among creamy lotus, and a chorus of bullfrogs strummed from deep in the marshes. A sleek anhinga broke water, flapping its powerful wings. "There is no better spot to observe them on the upper Texas coast," Bob said admiringly.

By day's end we had covered a lot of ground, and were debating the honors for most attractive summer bird. Doug had singled out the gallinules as "pretty hip." Bob chose the exquisite prothonotary warbler that had flashed behind the feathery willows. I had no favorite—I liked all of them.

White-tailed deer, swamp rabbits, and rare Russian boars also dwell here, and I saw all of them before I left. But Bob says that in winter, waterfowl are retreating to the less accessible areas; and he and other naturalists are concerned by the park's escalating popularity and the effect of that on animal life. More than 309,000 people, mostly Houstonites, passed through in 1985. Crowds arrive to bike, picnic, or stay overnight in one of 91 campsites. Weekdays, I watched fishermen roll by in the late afternoon and head for their favorite spots along the quiet creeks or at lighted piers along the lakes. An overabundance of alligators, however, precludes any wading, boating, or swimming.

"We didn't know how many were here when the state purchased the land," Superintendent Laird Fowler told me. Now he figures one gator for every four or five acres. The park has had to implement an "alligator nuisance program," removing troublesome animals to game farms.

One Sunday, while Laird and I were touring some of the remote trails, word came over the radio of another incident. A female had charged a fisherman who had climbed down a bank too close to her nest. Rangers roped off the site on Hale Lake, but before we got to it, someone had knocked down the barricade. The metal support poles had been pitched into the water, probably aimed at the mother. Laird retrieved one pole as she hissed at him—a sound, as an early naturalist noted, that "resembles very heavy distant thunder." Laird said the gator would have to go. The rangers would not disturb her forty-odd eggs, although probably no more than six hatchlings would survive predators. I asked him about relocating the animal in some backwater of the park. "Usually it isn't effective," he answered. "They find their way back sooner or later."

A veteran employee of the park, Frank Hoot, who grew up on these lands, believes that gators will usually avoid you unless they get accustomed to people and being fed by them. "I used to wade right next to alligators when I went frog hunting," he told me. But I definitely didn't want the park airboat to overturn when we cruised through the heron rookery on patrol. Hundreds of thousands of roseate spoonbills, herons, and white ibis were nesting in the yaupons, ashes, and willows. A sudden screech and a clash of jaws revealed the deceptive swiftness of the reptile: A baby bird lost its footing— and vanished in an alligator's maw.

Frank knows every bend in the trails and every duck in the air. He was foreman of a ranch here for thirty years, and has plenty of stories from the good old days. I heard some of them when he took me driving across Brazos Bend's 400 acres of "lone prairie." Summer's scant rainfall had turned them yellow, and patches of wild parsley, blue cornflowers, and red buckeyes begged for water. We were crossing the land where the ancient Capoques roamed; they were a group of Indians who probably moved inland from Galveston Bay. We lurched through the deep ruts worn down by wild boars beside the Brazos River, a sinuous blue smear along the park's eastern boundary. The flood of 1957 submerged all but ten acres of these bottomlands, Frank said. He doesn't expect Houston to impinge on wildlife here: "Too likely to flood, this countryside."

Laird Fowler suspects that changes are on the way. An impressive visitor center is nearly complete already. Other amenities have been proposed, such as golf courses and swimming pools. "But I don't think we'll put in anything that will change the nature focus of the park. Houston will expand this way in the next 15 to 20 years. We'll be the green jewel in the meadow of development."

Kentucky Horse Park

K entucky's bluegrass country resounds to the beat of hooves to this day. And in what other state would one expect to find a park devoted exclusively to the horse? Limestone formations of the region yield the minerals for strong bones, as seen in generations of champion Thoroughbreds. But not even plodding draft animals are scorned in the Kentucky Horse Park, a cluster of classic off-white farm buildings set in pastureland five miles outside Lexington.

KENTUCKY: NEAR LEXINGTON
1,032 ACRES

"It's really a public horse farm," executive director Lee Cholak told me—a place where "old-timers can get a kick out of seeing fields worked the way they remember." (Fresh produce, incidentally, is on sale at the adjacent campground, a resort complex with basketball and tennis courts, a swimming pool, and a laundromat.) The state has invested thirty-five million dollars in the park—not counting the cost of a new covered arena with 5,500 seats—and entrance fees help keep its grounds and buildings as tidy as the horses' manes. Even the trees appear symmetrical, and here staff members wear navy polo shirts and khaki pants instead of park-ranger green. "But this isn't Disney World," one official told me. "It's somewhere you can come and enjoy the beauty of the bluegrass and reflect on how horse and man built this world."

That ancient relationship is unfurled in the park's International Museum of the Horse. Ramps guide viewers through exhibits and dioramas as far back as 55 million years ago, when the "dawn horse" Eohippus roamed the earth. Splashy computer screens issue sports facts and other data on 63 modern breeds, while scenes from the Bayeux Tapestry supply state-of-the-art visuals for mounted warriors as of A.D. 1066. Quotations from Shakespeare, Zane Grey, and the Koran appear above murals of galloping horses on walls that, at the press of buttons, resound with whinnying and neighing.

"And God took a handful of southerly wind, blew his breath over it, and created the horse." That Bedouin legend suggests the admiration that fine horses can inspire, a mood that attracted visitors to local horse farms for years. In the 1970s, troubled by barn fires and liability insurance costs, the farms began turning visitors away; breeder John Gaines of Lexington envisioned a park as a substitute attraction. He took up the notion with state legislators, and by 1978 the old Walnut Hall stud farm had become a 1,032-acre park. Now champions John Henry and Forego are permanent residents, and other famous horses appear on loan.

Beyond the museum, up from the clanging of the farrier's shop, are the paddocks that house 33 breeds. Employee Tom Hamblen introduced me to miniatures named Nip and Tuck, to sleeker Arabians, and to Appaloosas with snowy muzzles. He pointed out the Icelandics, with straight blond manes that reminded me of Farrah Fawcett. Like the other stable employees, Tom has an obvious devotion to horses, and enjoys talking to the people who gather to touch, admire, or investigate suitable horses for a daughter or son.

"Bring your own mount" is a prerequisite for the semiannual Governor's Horse and Pony Weekend. Then young riders (and some over 18) gather for clinics in specialized skills of equitation. Before getting their own breakfast, they feed and clean their horses.

Cleaning stalls is the first lesson for students in the four-month course offered by the Kentucky Equine Institute, which uses the facilities here. Those admitted come from all over the world, says Kathy Hopkins, Director of Equine Operations, and some of them have never touched a horse before. They will study sound management principles, and may find careers on horse farms in the area.

I sampled lighter attractions. I saw the park's 20-minute film, *Thou Shalt Fly Without Wings*. Back in the sunlight, I watched riders in costume parading to the nostalgia of "My Old Kentucky Home." I paid my respects to the 11 broodmares, the great sire Rodney, and a pet dog in the cemetery up the hill—in central Kentucky, the tradition of burying a cherished horse is still respected. I stepped into a surrey with a fringe on top and let Marianne and Sparky—two Morgans—take me out in style; driver Charles Grote offered bits of information about famous animals and annual events as we clomped past Man O'War's statue (he's buried underneath).

On summer Sunday afternoons, players from the Lexington Polo Club gallop fast and furiously on their chestnut and gray ponies in exhibition games. As of late 1987 the United States Polo Association will be centered here, and seven additional fields are being added. I watched the Calumet Cup benefit matches, and thought the horses the most impressive performers of all. They appeared to need little guidance, finding their own cues and challenge in the quick turns and sudden halts. Spectators wandered in and out of a striped tent, and the scene suggested an afternoon in England—except that the visitors were eating ice-cold watermelon.

Tishomingo State Park

MISSISSIPPI: NEAR DENNIS
1,560 ACRES

O f Stephen Foster's songs, "Hard Times Come Again No More" would give a theme for Tishomingo State Park. In a bend off the historic Natchez Trace Parkway, this wooded retreat is one of ten in Mississippi that bear the imprint of the CCC—the Civilian Conservation Corps. Some three million youths served in the Corps, set up by President Franklin D. Roosevelt in 1933, until it was disbanded in 1942. In the desperate years of the Great Depression, it offered work—useful work—for the unemployed. They reforested lands, dug drainage ditches, built lodges and cabins. They left a rich legacy in national parks and forests across the country, and literally laid the foundation for many of our present state parks.

"They'd carry rocks right up on their shoulders, and their hands would be almost solid corns. But for me it was a good life," said retired minister James Blount. He was one of those who showed up for a CCC reunion at Tishomingo's handsome Loochapola Lodge. "I got the standard pay of $30 a month. But they let me work the gardens, so I got an extra $15." Blount had been a teacher in the camps, and he recalled teaching 18-year-olds to read and write—only two of the skills they learned that helped them earn a living when they got out.

Mildred Outlaw, once a camp laundress, and her husband, Artis, were there. So was David Quince Page. Camp comedian, he liked to spin yarns of the Model A Ford he kept concealed (illegally) among the trees for joyriding on Saturday nights. Until its discovery got him kicked out. Preacher Blount had been luckier with his escapades. "I sneaked out every night," he confided, "and rode my bike home."

Backslapping, joking, and reminiscences flowed on till suppertime; park manager Gary Ramsey had invited all the CCC veterans in the county. I heard them swapping tales of digging the Olympic-size swimming pool, sanding the floor of the lodge on hands and knees, forging iron lanterns for the cabins. (In 1936 the park planners had noted that because of the climate and the pesky insects, "persons staying overnight will undoubtedly want to get on the inside of a good tight house." They also thought that trailer camping would become popular as soon as paved roads came in—the closest pavement then was more than 50 miles away.)

After the others had left, Blount lingered awhile, exchanging gossip with Gary Ramsey and remembering the Tishomingo of his youth. He spoke of galloping after foxes, and of family get-togethers, still a popular Sunday-afternoon event here.

"We never realized how beautiful Tishomingo is until they turned it into a park. Then the people started commenting on it to us," he sighed. "It looks more like the Good Lord created it than any other park in Mississippi. So quiet, you can't even hear the trains clickety clacking." I wondered what brings him back these days. "My wife and I like to stroll along the old swinging bridge," he confided. "That's where we did our courting."

Built in 1940, the suspension bridge is a fine spot for looking down on Bear Creek, winding along from its spirited origin in Alabama to a placid course through Mississippi. Low-spreading branches of oak, cypress, and poplar shade its several milky brown miles inside the park, where it cuts through steep bluffs. Canoeists run with its currents, and fishermen cast from rowboats.

The stone fishing weirs along its banks were abandoned by the Chickasaw Indians when they were forced west to Oklahoma Territory in the 1830s. It was their famous chief Tishomingo who favored this area for hunting deer and bear. Local tradition says he especially liked Saddleback Ridge, where a stone arch and marker commemorate his people. I traversed the ridge on what seemed likely to remain an ordinary afternoon. Then a surprise thunderstorm blew in. The gusts swooshed through the aisles of skinny trees, sending shivers up my spine. I imagined Tishomingo: dark, handsome, giving a white child a ride on his spotted red horse. I imagined, too, a day in winter when leafless trees allow a panorama of Alabama's "Freedom Hills," a notorious haunt of outlaws.

The foothills of the southern highlands actually begin here, an area apart in a state generally flat. For visitors who drive up from the delta, says Gary Ramsey, "going to Tishomingo is like going to the Smokies." Sweet mountain camellias flourish here, as do wild azaleas, and the lobed spleenwort ferns crouch in deep crevices. Mountain folkways flavor local life, and for several days of the year the park hums to bluegrass melodies and the sawing and chopping of artisans at their craft.

One misty Saturday, Bertha Tidwell—mayor-elect of the town of Tishomingo—and I poked through tables piled high with white-oak baskets, handsewn quilts, and wooden bowls. We were serving as judges for the annual Bear Creek Folklife Festival, and finally we agreed on Mrs. Myrtle Aldridge and her clothesline of quilts for the best-of-show prize. Afternoon brought a slice of Mrs. Nevil Long's Mississippi mud cake, gooey and marshmallowy, and the whoops and hollers of buck dancers. Regrettably, I had to postpone buying the one item I coveted the most: a handcrafted dulcimer of the old southern Appalachian kind. In its haunting tones I always seem to hear the very spirit of the South.

Some thirty musicians jammed the lodge in the evening. Many plucked dulcimers of sassafras, cherry, or maple, with handcarved scrolls and pegs. Some strummed on banjos, while others kept the beat with wooden spoons. Many, I learned, could not read a note of music. Archie Lee sang humorously. Shirley Frye made magic on her Autoharp. And oh my, could these folks play! Nothing sounded more ethereal than the musical saw. As Charles Keys moved his violin bow across the smooth side of its specially tempered blade, the voices of angels seemed to float across the room. The foot-stomping, clapping, and improvising went on until well past midnight. I don't think I've ever encountered more fervor in a group, or a happier one.

And the music rolled again Sunday, "Dulcimer Day." Guests milled on the lawn, or sipped hot sassafras tea, or rocked on the lodge's wide veranda. There was the tinging of a 70-string hammered dulcimer, followed by the more fluid, flutelike tones from a courting dulcimer—one for duets. (Legend says that as long as the girl's father heard music in the parlor, the young lovers were not disturbed.) Skies darkened just as the group blended in a moving chorus of "Amazing grace, how sweet the sound. . . ." Bill Alexander announced: "That one's for you, Jane, to carry home to Virginia." Then came the soft rain, like gentle tears. I drifted off through their veil, exceedingly happy in heart.

I n the shadow of the Blue Ridge, in northwestern North Carolina, the rugged summits that local people call the Sauratown Mountains ring Hanging Rock State Park like the towers of a fortress. Within, waterfalls spill in gossamer sheets across dark gray ledges, and streams cluttered with scree purl through hillsides of pine, laurel, rhododendron, and dogwood.

Hanging Rock State Park

NORTH CAROLINA: NEAR WINSTON-SALEM
6,000 ACRES

Here the drama of the seasons is as noteworthy as across the way in the more touted Blue Ridge. Autumn brings its briskness to the throngs of backpackers, and swaths of red, russet, and gold to the crystalline creeks. By November most of the people have vanished for the unpredictable days of winter. Snowfalls bend the pines and mark the creases of high ground in white. Wildflowers cheer spring along, a time for wicker baskets and checkered cloths spread on tables and rocks. As spring bustles, so summer languishes. Families cluster at the bathhouse and 12-acre lake, leaving trails uncrowded. Vacant enough for me to hear the splatter of unexpected raindrops on the cinnamon ferns, to watch moss grow mossier, and to take in the view from the park's namesake outcrop with only a soaring bird for company.

I grew to like Hanging Rock in the dog days. I found escape from the heat and stuffiness in the plaintive breezes of the high country, in skipping stones in the shade of the creeks, and in splashing my face with their untainted waters.

One cloudless Sunday, I whiled away a few hours beside a den in the rocks—a lair 10 feet high, 12 feet wide, and 16 feet deep—with park employee Peg Martin and Jessica Howells, a ranger's wife. Close by, a two-stage waterfall plunged more than 200 feet, sidestepping quartzite terraces. We ate wild blueberries, and they told me a legend of the Revolutionary War.

British Redcoats didn't enter the area until late in the war, but local Tories did what they could for the Crown. They sought out these mountain caverns to stash food and munitions or to hide from the Patriots. In this particular den, the story goes, a band of Tories held the daughter of a Whig colonel named Jack Martin; they expected him to pay a generous ransom that could be used for the Loyalist cause. It was the girl's cleverness, people say with pride, that defeated them. Knowing that her father would be scanning the hillsides with a spyglass, she signaled for help by fluttering her petticoat. The flash of color was seen, and a rescue party set out immediately. Historians have refuted this tale—Colonel Martin didn't even have a daughter of the appropriate age—but people love to tell it anyway. "That's because it makes the Tories look so dumb," another Carolinian told me later. "Do you think anybody would repeat it if the Patriots had let a Tory girl run around waving a petticoat all over the place? Never!"

Independence Day, of course, was special, worthy of Mistress Martin and the colonel. When I arrived that morning just after 11 a.m., people were everywhere. From Raleigh, Greensboro, and Winston-Salem, they had come—4,020 in all when the park closed at 9 p.m. Hamburgers and hot dogs sizzled on grills, and throngs of squealing teenagers clustered around the two diving boards at the lake. I did some sunbathing, chatted with a number of families, ambled the trails.

Later I made my way to David Howells' house. He had arranged a night hike for campers, and Jessica and Peg Martin had planned a cookout for some friends. Graciously, they had included me, and I savored the hamburgers, assorted salads, and hot rolls. Around seven o'clock, when the wildflowers were less vivid than the dusty-rose sky, we left for the old fire tower on Moore's Knob, at 2,579 feet the park's highest ridge. We picked up a dozen campers from their tents and trailers.

Wisely, David had chosen the shorter of two trails. Even so, our climb was arduous enough. Still, we pushed on for 45 minutes, eager to see the grand display of fireworks from Winston-Salem, about 25 miles away. On the ridge, the gusts of wind were invigorating and the Blue Ridge vistas enchanting. Mauve, beige, then lavender shadows infiltrated the scarred slopes, turning the valley below into a dreamy seascape of mist. Skies turned charcoal gray, then black; off to the south, the city lights shined bright as beacons. Some of our party climbed to the top of the tower for the best possible view of the fireworks. A burst of color—one boom sounded, then another. And then the rising mists closed us off; for us, the show was over.

We had to console ourselves with the prospect of homemade vanilla ice cream, awaiting us at the Howellses'. Once, as we descended by the glow of flashlights and lanterns, I chanced to look back and saw an eerie display above me—thin beams of light rippling in the mist like streamers from party favors. Then I remembered the rekindling of the Statue of Liberty's torch for its centennial miles away in New York City. What a fitting celebration we had had. A state park. The Blue Ridge. Fine folks.

Bahia Honda State Recreation Area

As Marjorie Kinnan Rawlings said: "One man longs for the mountains . . . another man yearns for the valleys or the plains." And for another she knew, "Heaven . . . is a place of great waters." Surely he would have liked Bahia Honda (*bay*-uh, in local pronunciation). As its Spanish name suggests, it is a deep bay encircled by white beaches, with coconut palms swaying in the breezes. Its 328 acres complete a link in the Florida keys, a wonderland of waters. At Bahia Honda, time is immeasurable—there is always mañana.

Highway One cleaves the park as it winds south to Key West. A park road scoots past a beach, a marina, and camping sites on the Atlantic. A connector road swings under the highway to the Gulf side, sprinkled with more camper's coves and six stilt-legged cottages. Visitors have two spectacles for the price of one: sunset over the Gulf and sunrise over the Atlantic.

Renowned as one of the finest natural strands in the keys, the park's Sandspur Beach lures devotees from as far as West Palm Beach; they come to swim, scuba dive, snorkel, or windsurf, or just to relax. March brings the tarpon fishermen, July the lobstermen.

Usually uncrowded in summer, the off-season, the beach was rocking the evening I arrived with Raymond. A reggae band capped the first day of a windsurfing regatta. About sixty contestants had entered, and for two days their colorful sails would bob in the ocean as freely as kites. "Once you start windsurfing, you'll never look at any-thing the same way again . . . even a flag," a competitor explained. "You just look at how the wind's blowing it."

The wind didn't blow much the next day, and not at all the day after. But calm water and windless days are perfect for exploring the spectacular reef at Looe Key National Marine Sanctuary, 11 miles southwest of Bahia Honda. Here, as elsewhere in the nation, state and federal preserves complement each other and offer an agreeable choice of attractions. Raymond and I accompanied sanctuary ranger Bill Green on a routine patrol.

The Atlantic presented a shifting palette of blues that blistering July day, from turquoise to blue-green, then midnight blue in deeper spots. We moored at a buoy on the reef. Little remains of H.M.S. *Looe,* wrecked in 1744, but a scrap of metal from a recent wreck pokes out of the water and a sanctuary pamphlet cautions "Brown, brown, run aground." Where coral grows close to the surface, Bill explained, the clear waters look mud-brown. Grounding that damages the coral here can bring a fine as steep as $50,000, and in state waters the fine for injury to the reef goes as high as $10,000.

Water traffic was light that day. Only a handful of red flags, used to mark snorkelers and divers, fluttered on the translucent sea. I said something about the astonishing clarity of the water. "Oh, it can get even better than this," Bill replied. I peered straight down, about 15 feet, into a coral city: avenues of coral, running parallel to others of sand. With snorkel and mask, I could follow its surreal denizens: electric blue damselfish; gray-and-black angelfish; schools of sergeant majors swarming past broadly veined sea fans; a silver barracuda moving between weird brain coral and purple anemones. All was rhythmic, like a symphony without sound.

I never wearied of snorkeling at Looe Key or swimming, sun-bathing, and idling at Bahia Honda. One morning I would awaken early and wander along the Silver Palm Nature Trail. On another, I would wade at the water's edge, poking my toes deep in the sand as bits of coral swirled around them. In the evenings I would watch the sun dip into the glistening blue from my cabin balcony or from the old Bahia Honda Bridge. Beneath it lies the battered trestlework of Henry Flagler's overseas railroad, a developer's dream turned a folly by a 1935 hurricane.

I was never alone in observing sunset, for in the keys, this has al-most become a ritual. I recall in particular the evening aboard *Blue Angel IV,* when Raymond and I had spent a day off Bahia Honda and Looe Key with Captain Glenn Reber and first mate Scott Troy. We were about halfway back to the park when the sun's descent seemed to quicken into scarlet flame. Within minutes, the seas had doused it. A skyline of gold-dipped clouds thrust upward like the spires of a far-away magical kingdom. We toasted our day, then sailed onward into deepening darkness. I watched the moonlight shimmering off the bridge, and the heaven of twinkling stars. There was no whistling of trains. Only the circling of the sea gulls. The lapping of the waves. The rhythm of the head winds. No resemblance to the bluegrass beats, the purling of the mountain streams, or the whirring in the marshes. But it was music. More memorable stanzas in that wonder-ful chorus of southern parklands.

Lake Kissimmee
State Park

Patrol duty for Park Manager
Dave Randall includes an airboat
ride through 35,000-acre Lake
Kissimmee, merging point for the
park's other surrounding lakes
(Tiger and Rosalie) and headwaters
for the Everglades. Airboat searches
turn up an occasional poacher;
trespassers hunting on private land
caused a drop-off in deer and
wild turkey populations before the
preserve's establishment in 1970.
Remnant of a once extensive maze
of marshes, the lake nourishes
a variety of wildlife, such as
eagles, otters, and alligators.
The prairies—another Florida
resource safeguarded by the park—
also support abundant waterfowl.

Grasping an apple snail plucked from Lake Kissimmee, a snail kite alights on a post. Using its sharp, curved beak, it shells the mollusk swiftly. These kites, an endangered subspecies, all but vanished from their Florida range in the 1960s after widespread drainage of marshes killed off many of the snails they feed on. Perhaps 500 kites survive in the state.

FOLLOWING PAGES: A cow skull hangs from a post in a chickee, a shelter like those built by the Seminole Indians. Here, a ranger in frontier guise revives the 1870s for weekend visitors.

Brazos Bend
State Park

Serene woodlands, prairies, and marshes teeming with wildlife—all within an hour's drive of Houston—combine to make Brazos Bend one of Texas's most popular parks. Spring brings a special beauty to its 4,897 acres, as a sugar hackberry tree's buds flower among Spanish moss. Where pecans, elms, and oaks thrive along creek bottomlands, a ranger finds nesters from the park's 250 or so bird species. "In spring the whole place becomes a wildlife nursery," observes another ranger, Elaine Kenny (left), who befriends a three-week-old barred owl she rescued. Says Elaine, "you can't help falling in love with the place if you're here very long." Similar sentiments have brought thousands to the park since it opened in April of 1984.

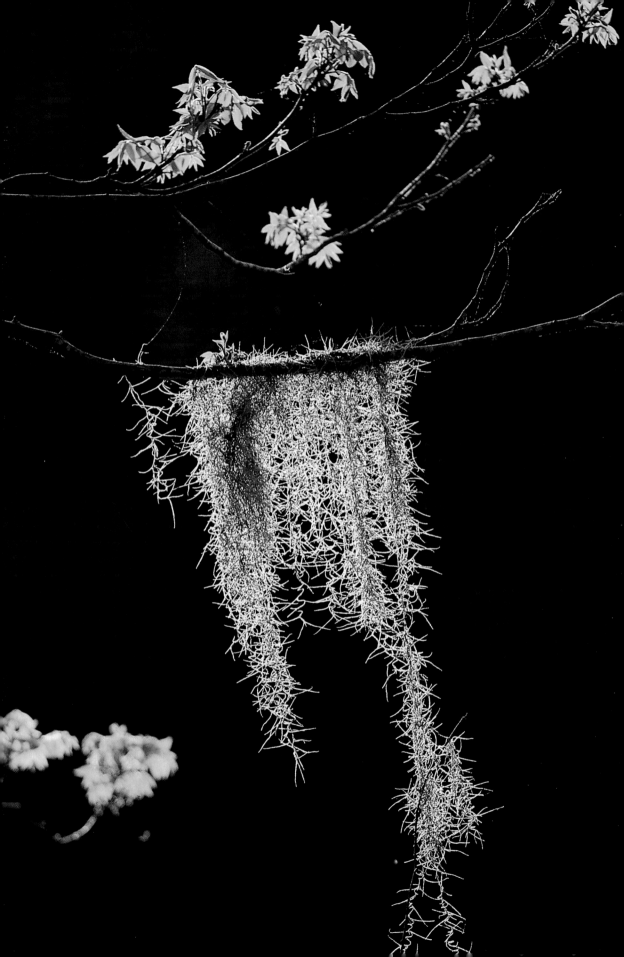

Trying his luck on a spring morning, an angler casts at Elm Lake, stocked with sunfish, crappie, bass, and catfish. Though intended for observers and photographers, wooden piers along some of the lakes also serve sportsmen, enabling them to fish where alligators make boating or swimming risky; officials estimate the current population at one six-footer for every four or five acres of water. "Though alligators . . . naturally repel us, they are not mysterious evils," wrote naturalist John Muir. Visitors consider them a major attraction. Trails crossing the marshes assure hikers of a glimpse or two of an animal draped with duckweed. Normally wary, the gators lose their fear when continuously offered handouts and turn aggressive when annoyed, a problem that gets worse as crowds increase. With caution signs throughout the park and a program to educate visitors, the staff hopes to avoid mishaps.

*Knee-high spider lilies—
Hymenocallis liriosome—bend in
the wind with sedges and rushes
thriving on a Brazos Bend tallgrass
coastal prairie. Beaded by morning
dew, the thin bracts radiating from
the flowers can reach lengths of
eight to ten inches, giving the plant
an overall width of as much as 15
inches. Brightening roadside
ditches in the Southeast, the lilies
bloom in spring; grasses blossom
in summer, turning the prairies
a straw color with fall's first frost.
Brazos Bend boasts the only
example of coastal tallgrass
prairie—about 400 acres of it—
among the Texas parks. Only
patches remain elsewhere
in the state: grazing lands and
urbanization have replaced them.*

Kentucky
Horse Park

Special park events let riders display and hone their skills. In the "Kentucky Challenge" for quarter horses, a racer tries to circle three barrels set 100 feet apart; a barrel knocked over costs a five-second penalty. Agility and speed also figure in summer's Sunday-afternoon polo matches, played by members of the United States Polo Association. Young equestrians eager to improve attend the Governor's Horse and Pony Weekend. Below, instructor Grace Greenlee shows a student just how to bathe her horse Radarlin after a trail ride. Of her first park visit, Grace says: "There's nothing like riding an Arabian in such a beautiful setting."

On loan as a fine example of his
kind, Zahara Zon—an 8-year-old,
15-hand Arabian—gazes over
the fence of a bluegrass paddock.
Arabian sires, of bloodlines refined
for 12 centuries, became the
foundation stock for all modern
Thoroughbreds: Kentucky's not
the least. Today, horses of 33 breeds
live or board at the park—"the
nicest place in the world for
horses," says one former employee.
Barns and pastures of the old
Walnut Hall stud farm hold the
animals; new facilities, including
restaurant, museum, and other
attractions cater to visitors.
Outlying fields encompass a four-
mile cross-country course called
one of the toughest in the nation.

Tishomingo
State Park

Celebrating spring: Swinging on a rope, Lee Hollingsworth grimaces as Bear Creek's chilly water splashes him. Nearby, on a stretch known as Horseshoe Bend, canoeists paddle beneath a canopy of river birches. From its turbulent origin in Alabama, Bear Creek glides quietly across northeastern Mississippi, past the limestone cliffs and dense forests of the hill country. The Civilian Conservation Corps built the park in the 1930s, quarrying area stone—known as Highland Church—for cabins and a lodge, and salvaging old cables from the Tennessee River for a suspension bridge that cost only $260. Now visitors come by car on the historic Natchez Trace Parkway, paralleling an old Indian trail.

Named for a Chickasaw chief, the park intrigues Mississippians from the delta country. "For them," notes the park manager, "going to Tishomingo is like going to the Smokies."

FOLLOWING PAGES: A father and daughter enjoy a leisurely Sunday horseback ride down Spring Hill, on Tishomingo's winding main road. Family get-togethers, lively bluegrass music festivals, and craft shows remain popular park pastimes, upholding cherished southern traditions.

Hanging Rock
State Park

Fed by spring rains, the Upper Cascades Falls stairsteps 100 feet. Climbing neighboring slopes between oaks and sassafras trees, catawba rhododendrons (above) flower at lower elevations in May, in higher reaches in summer. At right, blossoms swept downstream wedge against a broken branch. More than 300 species of plants thrive in the park, with Canadian and Carolina hemlocks side by side.

FOLLOWING PAGES: Its jagged brow overhanging 200 feet, park namesake Hanging Rock gives a panorama of the Piedmont's rolling countryside and the distant Blue Ridge Mountains. Table-mountain pines cling to its scarred surface, traversed by a solitary hiker.

Walking sticks come in handy for hikers Anna Carroll (at left) and Beth Anne Cooper, pausing briefly on rocky terraces below Hanging Rock. Largely quartzite, the heights locally called the Sauratown Mountains have resisted millions of years of erosion. Where softer sandstone or mica schist gave way, weathering left behind formations like the opening below, aptly named the Window. Its cracks and fissures fascinate young Tory Wagoner, exploring with a flashlight. Climbers often rappel from ridges along Moore's Knob. On a forested trail leading to it, sunlight highlights the spoke-like arrangement of the leaves of an umbrella tree, a mountain species of the magnolia family.

Bahia Honda
State Recreation
Area

Coconut palms bow to the Atlantic
along the southeast tip of Sandspur
Beach. Sun worshipers usually
lounge on the coral sands around
the bend from this point, empty at
sunrise except for seaweed and a
lobster trap washed ashore.
Possibly brought by wind and
water from the tropics, palms
mingle freely with native species.
Park policy calls for keeping
vegetation as it appeared in the
1600s when the Spaniards arrived,
so the staff removes Australian
pines. One storm-felled specimen
endures as a favorite perch for
frequent visitors like Jack and
Marcia Patrick from Key West.
Many Key Westers, they say,
drive the 36 miles to use this beach.
"It's the only public natural one
in the area," they add. Sunny days,
soothing breezes, and a casual
life-style also bring vacationers
from afar back to Bahia Honda
year after year.

FOLLOWING PAGES: Alone and
carefree, snorkeler Mercy Rozio
drifts in Bahia Honda's pellucid
waters, a paradise of tropical fish.
Park guests can bid farewell to
the day from a reinforced stretch
of the old Bahia Honda bridge,
a perfect spot to watch the sun
slip into the Gulf of Mexico.

NORTHEASTERN WOODS

AND WATERS

By Michael W. Robbins
Photographs by James P. Blair

Adirondack Park

The black water of Utowana Lake passage formed a dark mirror for the cloud-strewn sky, the overarching white pines, and the tamaracks on the banks. Guide Ernie LaPrairie pulled smoothly on his oars. "We're following the old steamboat route," he said. Steamboat? Some of these lake-to-lake passages seemed just wide enough for the oars of our guide-boat.

"They weren't very big steamboats," LaPrairie explained. "In fact, we'll see the last one to run on Blue Mountain Lake—the *Tuscarora*. Made her last run in the 1920s, and now she's being used as a summer cottage."

For LaPrairie, a guide for 20 of his 38 years, such lore came as naturally as his rowing. A cousin, Don Haischer, was purser on the *Tuscarora's* last trip, and an uncle—88-year-old Art Gates—had been an Adirondack fishing and hunting guide all his life.

For me, slipping along these tannin-tinted waters closed a circle begun in boyhood when I read the north woods adventures of "Nessmuk" (George Washington Sears) and others. I had fished lakes as black in forests as wild in Ontario and northern Wisconsin, but longed to traverse the great woods of the Adirondacks.

A mountain range, a region of upstate New York, and a forest preserve since 1885, the Adirondacks stretch the term "park" to its utmost. Encompassing some 9,375 square miles, Adirondack Park is far larger than most national parks (Yellowstone is 3,472 square miles), and is about the same size as the State of Vermont.

In many respects, it's like a state—one given over to outdoor recreation and wilderness. Voters amended the state constitution in 1894 to assure that the preserve "shall be forever kept as wild forest lands." In the 1970s the legislature created the Adirondack Park Agency and gave it power to guide and limit development on private lands. Now the park boundaries enclose a mosaic of public and private holdings, with 135 towns and hamlets. There are such renowned areas as Lake George and Lake Placid. The park boasts "great camps"—summer lodges built by America's wealthiest families—and 2,000 miles of hiking trails dotted with log lean-to shelters. The chain of lakes and rivers from Old Forge to Saranac Lake is a favorite route for canoes and guide-boats.

That's where we were, gliding easily on the black waters east of Raquette Lake, with Eagle and Blue Mountain Lakes still to cross. My wife, Wendy, our baby son, Patrick, and I rode in a pair of latter-day guide-boats. The guide-boat is a small craft peculiar to the Adirondacks, and its character suits the placid waters of the region as a ski does a snowy mountain.

Within the park boundaries lie 2,760 lakes and ponds. To explore

Nature's palette paints maples and white birches in blazing fall colors.
PRECEDING PAGES: *Three miles from the nearest road, hikers explore the Raquette River. Larger than any of the seven smallest states, the Adirondack Park offers wilderness to 60 million who live within a day's drive.*

them, you need a boat. Because the waters are separated by thick forest, you need a boat you can carry easily. That was true in the roadless years of the late 1700s and early 1800s when this region was settled by men given to hunting and trapping, and to logging and mining. It was true just after the Civil War, when recreational travel first boomed, and wilderness guides used boats to transport their clients. The guide would row and portage the boat and carry all gear, while the vacationer roughed it at his ease. Naturally the guides sought the lightest possible craft.

Thus was developed the Adirondack guide-boat: a narrow, round-bottom rowboat, handmade of local white cedar or white pine, and spruce roots. It attained its essential form by the 1850s and perfection around 1900. It cannot be reduced in weight without reducing its strength and carrying capacity. A 65-pound 16-footer that looks as fragile as a potato chip can carry two outdoorsmen and all their gear. It can be rowed swiftly or portaged for miles in comparative comfort. It is a tool that has become a work of art.

"The Adirondack guide-boat is the Stradivarius of small craft," says Ed Lynch, the first curator of the Adirondack Museum.

We put in for lunch in the cool shade of the cedars on Loonbrook Point, and LaPrairie told us it had been a firewood stop for steamboats. "My grandfather always said that the roads ruined the guide business," he added. Certainly roads made the Adirondacks more accessible to more people. But we had chosen to boat along the old routes because we wanted to see the north woods as they were seen by the early chroniclers of wilderness adventures. Obligingly, after lunch LaPrairie steered us up a side stream to a small but vigorous waterfall that was far from the nearest road.

We were riding in fiberglass boats with many of the virtues of the originals, but not their remarkable lightness. Some experts believe that "if it isn't wood, it isn't a guide-boat." But the surviving wooden boats have grown too valuable for commercial use. An original in good condition is worth about $5,000, while a new wooden boat from one of the few contemporary builders costs about the same.

"My grandfather sold his boats for $75 apiece," Jean Kerst told me as we walked among the displays at the Adirondack Museum, where he has charge of buildings and grounds. "He ran a sawmill down on Indian Lake, and was a guide. In the winters, he built boats—maybe 30 in his lifetime. One takes 300 to 400 hours of work."

To see where that time goes, we stopped at an exhibit of a guide-boat left partly assembled. It reveals that those thin cedar planks are not merely butted together, but that each has been hand-beveled on four sides to mate perfectly with its neighbors.

This museum, the very model of an effective regional museum, uses artifacts ranging from ornate private railroad cars to bumper stickers to convey the history of the Adirondacks, from the Gilded Age of the 1870s to the past decade's park zoning and land-use battles. Whenever we have come to the central Adirondacks in summer, we have started our explorations at the museum. With its campus of exhibits on a bluff above Blue Mountain Lake, it provides an overview of this vast region and park.

We completed our first water trip here (and our son's first-ever boat ride) by rowing around the islands and shores of Blue Mountain

Lake, watching for osprey, and catching glimpses of the timber and stone buildings of great camps as well as the piers and lawns of some venerable summer resorts.

"There's our room," Wendy pointed to a building all but hidden by tall trees. "Isn't that our balcony?" It was—the very balcony where on an earlier trip we had read and relaxed and watched the lake on a long summer evening.

On other occasions, in other seasons, we had approached the Adirondacks from different angles: Downhill skiing on Whiteface Mountain. Cross-country skiing on the wilderness trails around the rustic hotel spelled "Adirondak Loj" just south of Lake Placid. Climbing 3,759-foot Blue Mountain into a roadless wild forest. Staying and dining at that posh hotel "The Point," formerly William Avery Rockefeller's great camp at Saranac Lake. And just driving the scenic roads all the way down the center of the park from Tupper Lake to Great Sacandaga Lake.

But this time, when we returned to Ernie LaPrairie's boat shop at Steamboat Landing, I felt that the old guides were right, that the best way to see the Adirondacks is on the water. And I realized that with Ernie LaPrairie we had been in the company of a latter-day incarnation of the real north woods scouts and guides I had imagined when I was a boy.

Ridley Creek State Park

PENNSYLVANIA: NEAR PHILADELPHIA
2,600 ACRES

C hildren love this place." Jane Humphreys, director of interpretation at Colonial Pennsylvania Plantation—which is a living-history farm in Ridley Creek State Park, Pennsylvania—explained that they ran week-long summer workshops for children. "It's not like school, though. It's more like day camp." Remembering some manic spotted piglets, I asked what the children liked best.

"The chores," said Humphreys. "Their favorites are cooking and cleaning. Doing the morning chores with the animals, feeding the chickens and gathering eggs."

In short, what 20th-century children like most about this 18th-century farm is the work. . . .

On the 20th-century side of Ridley Creek, I asked Superintendent Franklin Haas about the most popular activity there.

"Other," he said. On a questionnaire that lists hiking, picnicking, fishing, horseback riding, bicycling, Nordic skiing, playing ball, most people answer "other." Haas went on: "What that means is just hanging out. Just people driving in here to sunbathe or walk around, or read."

Working. And hanging out. This park can accommodate a long span of interests. It has to—it draws a million visitors a year. Ridley Creek is a large, varied, open and green space in a densely populated region. It's about 15 miles west of central Philadelphia, and it provides respite from urban brick and neon and concrete.

This day-use park gets its share of urban problems: vandalism, drug use, disorderly conduct. Law enforcement is one of Haas's major headaches, though I never saw anything that signified trouble.

Park headquarters is housed in a splendid mansion built in 1914 by the Jeffords family. (It was they who assembled these green acres from a cluster of small colonial farms and preserved them as Philadelphia suburbs grew around them; the holding was purchased by the state in 1965.) Even with Ridley Creek's mansion, formal gardens, deer herd, and trout stream, Haas answered "no" when I asked if his job was considered a plum. It's not just the lack of staff for law enforcement, he said. There's a lot of wear and tear on a park so heavily used, and not enough money to maintain it as Haas would like.

Still, Ridley Creek is meeting real needs for large numbers. And no wonder. This is a beautiful place, with long bike paths under arching sycamores; open fields for kite flying or dog training; a clean rocky creek for wading; shady spots for lunch hours; and two historical enclaves: Sycamore Mills, managed by the park, and the Colonial Plantation, administered by a nonprofit group.

Sycamore Mills is the remnant of an 18th- and early 19th-century industrial village. It had a gristmill, a sawmill, a rolling mill (for iron), and a nail factory, all powered by the waters of Ridley Creek. Some buildings burned in 1901, leaving walls now draped with vines; others stand intact, and are rented out to residents. Sycamore Mills shows the scale and purpose of a real community, an industrial complement to the agricultural plantation.

There the gritty, everyday story of late colonial days is alive and in motion. This is a real 112-acre farm with a stone farmhouse, stock pens, a springhouse for cooling milk and butter, and gardens producing vegetables and herbs. What goes on here is a facsimile of rural life, replete with hard work, slow pace, and dirt. What also goes on is painstaking research, mostly by volunteers.

"What we're doing is recovering some lost lessons from history," says resident farmer Jim Nichols. Knowledge needed for everyday farming was rarely written out, but was passed by word of mouth—or was lost once that oral chain was broken. So Nichols, who grew up on a farm in central Pennsylvania, is working to rediscover ways and means that his predecessors would've known as a matter of course: when exactly to plant corn, how exactly to dock the tails of lambs.

Moreover, everyone at the Plantation works as an interpreter—not reciting memorized lines or staging episodes, but living 1760s style. If you stop in at mealtime, you'll see the family and hands sit down and eat an authentic 18th-century farm supper, cooked over a fire in the kitchen's cavernous fireplace. Or you may see Nichols slopping the hogs, or someone else pulling flax. And if you want to know more about the old ways of doing these tasks, they'll tell you what they've learned.

On a hot day, I watched the farmworkers doing chores. They went barefoot, but their clothing looked heavy and hot. And grubby. Cinny Goldwater, the volunteer farm manager, told me that one of the questions children ask frequently is, "Why are you so dirty?" It's because there was no time—what with making soap from animal fats and ashes, and drawing water bucket by bucket from the well, and bringing it to a boil over an open fire—to wash clothes very often. And, Cinny added, "English colonial laborers didn't bathe."

It's an authentic place, chores and all.

I t may be true that only God can make a tree, but man can make a
forest park. Watoga State Park in southeastern West Virginia
demonstrates that parks don't just happen, but are created
through vision, plain hard work, and years of loving care. First
and largest of the Mountain State's many parks, Watoga occupies
10,000 acres of steep ridges and coves along the Greenbrier River.
When we first drove its lone, narrow road, we commented on the unbroken denseness of the oak and maple forest.

"It looks as if it's always been heavily wooded," I said.

But this is, in fact, recent growth. "All the timber was pretty well
gone by the turn of the century," Superintendent Walt Shupe told us
later. The ravaged land was reforested during the late 1930s by the Civilian Conservation Corps. Hundreds of men planted trees, cut trails,
built roads and a dam and a swimming pool. Best of all, the CCC fel-
lows built and furnished the log cabins that are the pride of this state
park system.

Log cabins suit these deep Appalachian coves. They were crafted of chestnut logs, based on stone quarried in the park. Cool and
dim inside, sharply scented by woodsmoke from their blackened fire-
places, most of Watoga's 25 "standard" cabins are unique in plan, as
individual as their random-width plank floors. Each contains fit-
tings—rough-hewn chests and tables, hardware blacksmithed from
discarded wagon rims or railroad rails—as individual as the men
who crafted them.

I wish I had known this park when I was 12 years old and fascinated by characters like Daniel Boone, and Hawkeye, and Indians.
My parents could have relaxed at the cabin while I scouted the trails
in a real forest roamed by real deer and black bear. It would have
seemed simply too good to be true.

These cabins are perfect for family getaways without the bothers
of camping. In midsummer, my wife, Wendy, wanted us to bring
baby Patrick and stay in one of the eight two-bedroom "deluxe" cabins, built in 1955. Each has pine-paneled walls, a large stone fireplace
(split hardwood is furnished), oak floors, and homemade wood
sconces and table lamps. Also a small furnace (nights are cool, even
in June), a tiled shower, and a well-equipped kitchen.

"This would be a wonderful place to meet friends for a holiday,"
I said.

"*You,*" said Wendy with emphasis, "could cook a full Thanks-
giving dinner right here." I reminded her that nobody has to cook
here: Hearty meals are served at the park's knotty-pine coffee shop.

We took note of the park's tempting choices—the stable of horses for trail riding, the stocked lake with rental boats, the tennis courts,
even the game room. We elected to hike the trails.

One afternoon, we followed a loop called the Honeymoon Trail
that dropped down from a high saddleback ridge. Partway down, we
stopped to feed Patrick, and saw some decayed split-rail fence an-
gling across the forest floor—a holdover from one of the hardscrabble
farms that hung on until creation of the park. " 'Garden' farms," Walt
Shupe called them, with "just a cabin and a garden patch, and maybe
a barn with a few animals" on the cut-over hills. "Folks were just ek-
ing out a living." Only the fences remain from these homesteads—
"and there are a few gravestones out there."

Watoga State Park

WEST VIRGINIA: NEAR MARLINTON
10,000 ACRES

From the ridgetop clearing where we'd parked our car, the view to the west was across the Greenbrier River to the Monongahela National Forest. Behind us to the east, the ridges and valleys ran in long north-south parallels. But to the west, that order broke down into the random ridges and dead-end hollows of Appalachia: hazy, overlapping triangles of wooded hills. It struck us that this breezy ridge with its grassy clearing was ideal for a picnic.

The next evening, we returned with fried chicken, potato salad, rolls, and coffee. As the sun eased down in a pale orange haze over the shadowed ridges in the west, a full moon—ripe and creamy—loomed up behind the oaks on the east side. We stayed in the rustling silence until the sun was gone, Patrick was asleep, the moon was high, and the breeze had grown chilly.

Superintendent Shupe gave us a pickup-truck tour of the park one day, from the Beaver Creek Campground on the east ("one of the first campgrounds in the state") to the new 50-site Riverside Campground on the west. "It's hard to maintain a 50-year-old park," he said; "it's a struggle to get the money to do the job right." But he explained how quickly his crew—plus hired hands, and even some convicts—had cleaned up the fallen trees and restored the amenities after the disastrous flood of November 1985. When he proudly showed us the seamless repairs to some of those 50-year-old cabins, we concluded that the condition of this park owed much to his energy and determination.

We tried a trail he recommended: a gradual climb up a fire road to the Ann Bailey Overlook, a prolonged descent on Jesse's Cove Trail to the east bank of the Greenbrier River. With Patrick bouncing happily in his backpack, we hiked down through a long-uncut forest into a deepening cove. With mossy banks and masses of blooming rhododendron, the trail wound under a silver-green canopy that rippled and flashed in afternoon sunlight. Plumb-straight tulip trees, red oaks, maples, and birches rose up from the steep-sided cove. We saw fresh prints of deer, and twice we heard them dashing up the slope. The trail crossed and recrossed the gray boulders of Rock Run, and all the while we hiked down in the shifting, dappling sunlight, a cooling current of air flowed up past us.

Near the end of our hike, where the sunlight was reflecting up from the surface of the river, we rested on a bank of leaves and moss. Wendy held Patrick and fed him his bottle, and we enjoyed a forest silence broken only by his eager gurgles. Then Wendy whispered: "Did you hear that?" Scratching sounds, as of some laborious effort.

I looked around—perhaps a raccoon?—and hoped I wouldn't see a bear. Wendy pointed straight down. Between us, a tuft of moss moved, lifted, and dropped. We watched a small part of the earth move, the surface grasses and seedlings swaying. Some small animal was burrowing just beneath the surface. The movements increased. We waited for a small nose to poke into the daylight. Alas, Patrick became so noisy that the movements stopped abruptly. After some seconds, there was a final trembling among the leaves and moss, then stillness.

Whatever it was must have heard us, and decided to surface at another place, another time.

Watoga—once barren—is full of life.

N iagara Reservation, established in 1883, is now the oldest state park in America. (Yosemite, entrusted to California by Act of Congress in 1864, was ceded back to the federal government in 1906.) Niagara Falls was the first American natural wonder to win world attention, and the first to attract travelers on a large scale. And the falls inspired one of the first conscious, organized, political decisions to wrest a natural wonder from private exploiters and preserve it with dignity as a public trust. At the dedication ceremony in July 1885, a state official declared: "from this hour, Niagara is free." He meant that henceforth no one need pay to see the falls, and that they were liberated from an entourage of—as a disgusted visitor said—"fakirs and extortionists." "The admission to Goat Island was fifty cents," reports a historian, "and to the Cave of the Winds, one dollar. To gain Prospect Park . . . twenty-five cents." Every vantage point had its price—a high price, in years when a workingman was lucky to earn two or three dollars a day.

Moreover, the majesty of Niagara was compromised by industrialists who tapped the water power for unsightly riverbank paper mills, sawmills, cereal factories, and gasworks. Hackers, "guides," peddlers, and pitchmen with five-legged calves or "astonishing reptiles" to show were equally bent on tapping the pockets of visitors.

Public protest against all this helped bring our oldest state park into being. Thus an attitude we now call "respect for environment" first managed to eclipse the P. T. Barnum in our soul.

Today Niagara Reservation, designed by Frederick Law Olmsted of Central Park renown, retains the air of a pleasantly aged city park: artfully landscaped, with lawns and flowers, trees and shrubbery and benches. Access to the falls remains free, and simple.

To reach that free and tranquil public zone, we drove along a congested and rather forlorn commercial strip, U.S. 62, that fed into downtown Niagara Falls. The tourism trade remains brisk and competitive, and the city of Niagara Falls—hit hard by rust-belt economic reversals—is a welter of parking garages, fast-food outlets, high-rise motels, and shops selling "Indian" souvenirs. Still, that's only a faint, almost nostalgic echo of the commercialism that surrounded the falls before 1885.

Transcending such lily-gilding touches as colored floodlights at night, the falls themselves continue to thunder away: 170 to 180 feet high, a 700,000 gallons-per-second daytime flow of flying, foaming whitewater. I had seen them once before, when I was ten years old, in early winter. Then, partly rimmed in ice, they seemed too powerful to be endured, as if they might reach out and sweep me away.

I remember that my mother watched the cascading water for a while, then wondered aloud if it might be turned off at night. Then the notion did not seem odd. The falls were too much: too vast, too noisy, too high, and surely there was too much water pouring over those final edges. Surely Lake Erie would be emptied. Surely that much water could not be falling continuously. I seem to remember that the falls made me think about the meaning of "forever."

That sense of something truly overpowering is a constant at the falls. You do have to see them; it is impossible to imagine that much water falling and falling, to imagine the dizzying sense of mortality and of the world's sublime indifference.

Niagara Reservation State Park

NEW YORK: AT CITY OF NIAGARA FALLS
435 ACRES

Above all, it is thrilling and sobering to stand so close to so inhospitable a wonder of nature. Few of us get to stare into an active volcano or into the teeth of a white shark in the surf and survive to explore our feelings about it. But at Niagara Falls, one can stand near the brink and know one could not survive that plunge, and then turn and go about one's own business.

I remember the falls of my childhood seeming larger, rougher, noisier; and those impressions are valid. Today, less water is falling. At night and during the winter, some 40 percent of the flow of the Niagara River is diverted for hydroelectric generation. Coincidentally, that diversion serves to slow the rate of erosion—and thus to conserve the spectacle itself. My mother was onto something: They don't shut it off at night, but they do turn it down.

Camel's Hump State Park

VERMONT: IN THE GREEN MOUNTAINS
19,474 ACRES

When I reached the bare summit of Camel's Hump, seven other backpackers were sunning on the weathered gray schist. Here, in good summer weather, on a weekend day, a crowd is 20 or 25 people. It's not that this Vermont peak is ugly or unpopular. Rather, it's all but unknown outside the state and the fellowship of hiking.

Camel's Hump itself, the 4,083-foot summit, is no secret. It juts above tree line and can be seen from miles away. But as I drove toward it, I saw no park signs. My map showed no visitor center, not even an entrance.

In Huntington, a nearby town, I stopped at a general store and asked for directions. I read from my map, naming local landmarks.

"Nope," said the man at the register. "Don't know any Honey Hollow. No Robbins Mountain, neither."

According to my map, Huntington lay nearly in the shadow of Robbins Mountain. Never heard of it?

A customer said he hadn't known of a park up there.

Maybe this was some Yankee woodchuck humor of the "You-can't-get-there-from-here" school. I consulted a young man who was scraping old paint from the clapboard sides of the post office. He politely gave me instructions for going back where I'd come from.

I decided to try every dirt road leading toward the peak, and finally came to Brautigam's Nordic Ski Center; they directed me to a trailhead with, at last, a sign: "Camel's Hump State Park."

Working my way up a narrow trail that soon turned as rocky as a stream bed—and nearly as damp—I learned another reason why this mountain was uncrowded: Once found, it's hard to climb. The trail clambered over knee-high root terraces and loose rocks, slithered on mud ruts and mossy stone. As I backpacked up through a forest of sugar maple, paper and yellow birch, and beech, I waited for the ground and air to dry at higher elevations. Nothing dried out. I climbed alongside spattering, impatient brooks. Later, forestry district manager Jim Cronin told me that Camel's Hump gets a lot of moisture from mist, rain, and snow: the equivalent of some 85 inches a year, which is more than New Orleans gets.

I knew I would be ascending through three life zones, counting the alpine tundra atop Camel's Hump; climatologically speaking, that's like hiking in one day from New England to, say, Labrador. I hoped to reach the summit before sunset, and hoped the sky would be clear (it seldom is, on New England's cloud-snaring alpine peaks).

In summer, Camel's Hump offers "primitive" campsites; three "lodges," or small cabins; and two tent platform areas, each with eight sites. "Primitive" camping in Vermont means no-trace camping out of sight of any trail. It's allowed in Camel's Hump, but not above 2,500 feet—and I wanted to get up to 4,000 for the view.

Abruptly, I stepped into a room-size clearing where a wooden sign announced that another four-tenths of a mile remained to the top. I shed my backpack and walked lightly, noting the effects of the alpine climate. The firs dropped to shoulder height, then waist height, then down to dense krummholz, or "crooked wood." Then the wind found only a mat of ground-hugging greenery to stir.

Much of the ten-acre summit clearing was bare rock, on which daubs of paint blaze a trail. Signs caution hikers to stay on the rock to avoid trampling the slow-growing alpine plants. Obediently, all eight of us present were sprawled on the rocks.

Filling all the thin soil among the sun-warmed rock, the alpine tundra looked neat as a Japanese garden. I dropped down prone to examine the dwarf willow, and the mountain cranberry that resembles a succulent, and the Bigelow's sedge. I wished I had remembered to bring a loupe or a magnifying glass; these tiny sedges and various berry plants represented a geographic reach far longer than my view of the Green Mountains. I stayed on top until I began to stiffen from the afternoon's climb. (The alpine plants are right; it's better to stay down out of the wind.)

Descending, I thought of late September when the maples and birches would become a fiery mosaic. Now the trail looked steep as a fire escape dropping away in the dripping twilight.

Suddenly I came upon Gorham Lodge, the Green Mountain Club shelter nearest the summit; a wash pit, then a log bridge across a welcome spring, then a log cabin shored with boulders against a ledge. It was small—16 by 20 feet—and basic. Four campers were already there and one said the caretaker, Ellen Bauman, would return. While I was talking with Stan Lucas from Norwich, Connecticut, who was backpacking with his son Mason, three more sweating hikers trooped in. I was dubious that nine people could sleep here, and I had counted on tenting in solitude.

However . . . the sun was going down, a fog was easing in among the pointed spruces, and Lucas told me the nearest tent platform was 1.2 miles farther down. The pluses of a hut came clear: It's sited near reliable springs; it's roofed against the rain; it's screened against mosquitos and flies; it should deter the black bears said to be common here (two orange eastern newts were all the fauna I'd seen yet). And the company was welcome—and welcoming.

We introduced ourselves: Mason, Wendell, Steve, Ellen, Stan, Mike, Ray, John, Paul. I traded some of my real, ground coffee for the use of a stove already hot, and cooked my supper.

Wendell and Stephen Morrison, teenage cousins from nearby, had hiked here before and were able to pinpoint on my map some of the features, like Robbins Mountain (no relation), which had eluded my "guides" down in Huntington. The 'packers (club rugby team-mates in Washington, D.C.) were Paul Sheehy, John Bosley, and Ray Thomas. Seasoned campers, they were enjoying a last hike together before Bosley entered law school. He described the stretch of the state's Long Trail they had covered that day: "very up and down."

We selected our spaces on the wooden platforms and rolled out our sleeping bags. The fog brought an early darkness. Candles spread a glow from the table where the teenage boys began telling stories. Just outside, in the soft, dripping night, Stan offered good cigars to everyone and we talked about other mountains and other parks, and where we lived and what we did. I asked Paul Sheehy about his work and he said he was a doctor, a "research doctor."

And the nature of his research?

"Cancer," he said. "Some ways to combat cancer." Then he explained, patiently and in layman's terms, the paths he was exploring and how they might lead to cures.

Listening, and becoming drowsy, I thought about the life close around us, about the short time we had, and about the wonder of this company choosing to spend some of their time in such a wild, dark place—of meeting once and sharing this secret mountain park, and then heading out again to such different lives.

There's a reason to work your way in to such a remote place: to see who else is there.

Then we turned in.

Franconia Notch State Park

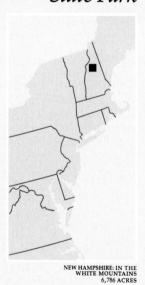

The more you walk, the more you'll see." That's what the park ranger said when I asked about the foot trails up to the Flume, a geological attraction in Franconia Notch State Park, in New Hampshire's White Mountains. He was referring to the route to the Flume, but he characterized the entire park.

The notch—that's what New Englanders traditionally call a mountain pass—is a narrow, rock-bound channel between the Franconia Range on the east and the Kinsman on the west. Shaped by a glacier, its rough-hewn beauty has drawn visitors since the 1830s, and it seems to have a special appeal to New Englanders: Ralph Waldo Emerson wandered here, Nathaniel Hawthorne wrote about it in his story "The Great Stone Face," and Robert Frost once owned a house just to the north. The notch now serves as a route for human travel; Interstate 93 takes up much of the valley floor.

This is one park that can be seen from an auto. You can scan the forest and the flanking slopes of the mountains that rise 1,000 to more than 3,000 feet above the road. You can see the park's most striking feature, 1,200 feet above Profile Lake, the stern-faced rock formation known as the "Old Man of the Mountain"—long regarded as symbolic of the granitic strength of all New England.

You may catch a glimpse of the red or yellow cars of the new aerial tramway which—in all seasons—swing up the side of Cannon Mountain to 4,000 feet, below the summit on the northeast side. They'll give you a floating, wide-angle view of the notch, Eagle Cliff, some of Cannon's ski slopes and trails, and nearby peaks.

But, as the ranger said, if you really want to see it, you've got to get out and walk. Or, rather, hike.

That's what we did. For those—like Wendy and me—keen on day-hiking, on traveling light in the forest, in the northerly air and the welcome silence, Franconia offers a tracery of mountain trails. We plotted a route for a day of carrying a lively six-month-old: riding up in the morning, working our way down via the High Cannon Trail, the Dodge Cutoff, and the Lonesome Lake Trail. Often, when we started down through balsam fir and spruce, young Patrick could clutch at boughs with either hand. He floated along, watching the play of sunlight through the green. We picked our way over a tangled fretwork of raised roots trimmed in star moss—one of those basic Appalachian granite-and-schist trails. If you don't wear stiff-soled shoes you'll feel you spent the day walking on upended spades.

Later, we followed the ranger's advice and walked up through the Flume. It's a notch in miniature, some 800 feet long, 12 to 20 feet wide. A swift-running stream—still at work—routed it down through layers of rock. A wooden walkway angles up through the Flume, against its mossy granite walls. Dusky light filters down from the forest floor overhead, and the cut is filled by the rushing of foamy whitewater. It's an easy half-mile walk among constantly watered, brilliant green ferns and mosses and wood sorrel.

Withal, we found Franconia Notch reminiscent of New England itself: full of surprisingly varied assets in a modest-size area. Mountain peaks, pools, waterfalls, and wild forests—in just 6,786 acres. Echo Lake, near the base of Cannon Mountain, has a popular beach—and enough breeze for board-sailors. Between Echo Lake and Artists Bluff, there's a series of Nordic ski trail loops. And the park is ingeniously threading a bike path through the cramped notch, beside the Pemigewasset River.

It was ice that shaped the notch, and ice—freezing and melting through the long winters, in autumn and spring—that sculpted the "Old Man" whose dour profile presides over this White Mountain fastness, and who seems to personify one facet of New England's character: its gritty endurance.

To savor another facet—an old-fashioned feel for doing things right—we turned to another of Franconia's surprises: the store of the League of New Hampshire Craftsmen. The building itself is a statement about the virtues of plain materials beautifully assembled. Inside, there's a rich variety of quality objects in wood, wool, silver, ceramic, and glass: clever toys, handsome clothes, and useful kitchenware—all created by the people of the Granite State.

The care that was evident in every object reminded us at once of the Adirondack guide-boats and the sturdy cabins of Watoga. It struck us that in all these state parks is a genuine, lively tradition that flowers at times as craftsmanship but is rooted in some deeper cultural bedrock: a love of the country, a sense that these are special places with their own history and their own beauty; and a proud determination not merely to preserve these places but to improve them. These parks reflect something strong and wonderful in the people who are committed to them. It is not a kind of thing an Ernie LaPrairie or a Jim Nichols would speak about, but it's there.

Call it character.

Adirondack Park

Early morning mist rises from Blue Mountain Lake as Ernie LaPrairie holds an Adirondack guide-boat at a stand of white birch and cedar trees. Among the first settlers here, members of LaPrairie's family have

used "the Stradivarius of small boats" since the 1860s. Sturdy enough to withstand harsh conditions, yet light enough to be carried by one person, the guide-boat became the primary means of transportation in the area. "My mom used to row to school," says LaPrairie. A handful of craftsmen like Ralph Morrow continue to make the boats out of local white pine and white cedar, with spruce roots for the ribs. "All I've ever done is work on boats," says Morrow, who spends about six weeks on each at his home in Saranac Lake. Morrow's boats currently sell for $5,500 apiece; a new guide-boat in molded fiberglass costs about $1,300.

Visible from 30 miles, Mount Marcy crowns the Adirondack Mountains at 5,344 feet. The summit, worn round by time and weather, rises behind a two-seat floatplane. These planes specialize in transporting hunters and sportsmen to certain designated lakes. More than 40 summits rise higher than 4,000 feet in this "high peaks" region of the park, largest of its 15 wilderness areas. Master plans define nine categories of state-owned land, six of private holdings. Privately owned land, including vast stretches of forest, makes up 62 percent of the total within the "blue line," or park boundary. The Adirondack Park Agency administers land-use policy, weighing community needs, historic values, and primeval realities of wild country.

Ridley Creek
State Park

Fifteen miles and two hundred years away from downtown Philadelphia, the Colonial Pennsylvania Plantation in Ridley Creek State Park re-creates life on a working farm in the late 18th century. Interpreters at the Plantation, dressed in faithful reproductions of colonial clothing, work the farm using the tools and techniques popular from the 1760s through the 1790s. With a tool called a swift, Jean Yarsawich winds yarn into a ball for knitting hats, shawls, and gloves worn by the interpreters. Wool for the yarn comes from sheep raised on the Plantation along with pigs, chickens, and cattle. Children play a rousing game of tag in front of a farmhouse built before 1710.

Several major additions during the following 130 years have given the building its present size and form. Besides playing games, these young volunteers find kindling, slop the hogs, and gather the hens' eggs. Their counterparts 200 years ago would have had to hunt for the eggs, since chickens—like sheep—roamed free. These "dunghill" fowls did not belong to any named breed; the Dorset sheep and the red Devon cattle came from hardy English strains.

Watoga
State Park

Clear water gently flows among moss-covered boulders where erosion and decay once reigned. Rock Run (left) curves through a forest of oak, maple, and birch trees logged barren by 1920. Woodlands in Watoga State Park today reveal the mastery of the Civilian Conservation Corps reforestation program from the 1930s. The CCC also reintroduced wildlife into the park, including deer, raccoons, and turkeys. Here a wild turkey hen walks near the trail leading to a lookout tower. A four-foot black rat snake, one of the largest nonpoisonous snakes in the U.S., flicks its tongue at an intruder.

FOLLOWING PAGES: Created by the CCC in 1935, 11-acre Killbuck Lake offers boating, canoeing, and other water sports to Watoga's summer visitors. West Virginia anglers flock to the lake in March, April, and May to fish for stocked trout —rainbows, browns, and brookies.

Niagara Reservation State Park

Such views as these—of Bridal Veil Falls (left) and the expanse of American Falls (below)—lie safely in the public domain, thanks to the establishment of America's oldest state park a century ago. Through most of the 1800s tourism and industry befouled the site with tawdry hustlers and squalor— "a new fee for every point of vantage," noted one historian, and "manufactories" extending "to the brink of the Falls." Then, at the park opening on July 15, 1885, an orator proclaimed: "From this hour Niagara is free." Visitors today enjoy free access to Prospect Park beside the falls and to the islands that divide the cataracts; the state levies fees for parking and for the tour that ends on tempestuous Hurricane Deck, 20 feet from Bridal Veil, as close as anyone can get to the bottom of the falls on the American side. Below, the view from Prospect Point sweeps across American Falls to narrow Luna Island, then Bridal Veil and broad Goat Island, to Horseshoe Falls and the Canadian side. A large volume of water and the wind pattern give Canada a grander cloud of mist. "Ours," counters a spokesman for the New York park system, "makes better rainbows."

Camel's Hump State Park

Around its largest state park, Vermont has created a forest reserve to maintain the traditional rounds of rural life and its timeless look—the hard-edged seasons, the ponds and wooded hills, the dirt roads and farmsteads, a dozen villages with their shaded white colonials. Much of the Camel's Hump Forest Reserve, like frozen Gillett Pond with its naked sentinel birches, remains in private hands. Within the reserve the 19,474-acre park rises to the distinctive double summit of Vermont's "best-loved" mountain, famous, high, and still undeveloped. "A promise was made to this mountain," proclaims a state agency, "That the only changes it would undergo are Spring, Summer, Fall, and Winter." Yet recent decades have brought other changes, with a troubling decline in forest density. Has acid rain caused it? Researchers pore over the mountain, seeking answers. Vermont has promises to keep.

Glaciers profiled the mountaintop (left) into . . . *The Mountain That Is Like a Seat,* said the Indians. *Le lion couchant—reclining lion,* thought the explorer Samuel de Champlain. *Camel's Rump,* noted Ira Allen, brother of Ethan, on the map he made in 1798. Victorian eyes, uplifted, beheld *Camel's Hump.* Under the snowy dome sleep 11 tundra plants rare in Vermont—and fully protected by the park. In the forest reserve (below) skiers track a groomed trail in a privately owned area, passing a plantation stand of young spruce.

Franconia Notch State Park

"There is a right hardness on the side of New Hampshiremen with which they face the world." So noted an essayist, and so appears the state emblem—the granite ledges that compose the Great Stone Face of Franconia. The essay also reflected the lasting warmth of Granite State friendships: "It is granite that holds longest after nightfall the heat of the sun." Before winter descends, the Franconia heights (above) glow with the warm autumn hues of the hardwoods. Nearby, a covered bridge offers a spot from which to contemplate the Pemigewasset River (left), and the geological pothole known as the Pool.

JOSÉ AZEL (ALL)

85

FRANCONIA NOTCH STATE PARK 2

Tramming or tramping? Either way leads to Cannon Mountain's summit above Franconia Notch. The aerial tram—successor to a 1938 model, first passenger tramway on the continent—lifts 80 tourists or skiers 2,000 feet in six minutes. Backpacking up at an easy pace might take two and a half hours. Here the vista spreads from Kinsman Mountain across the notch to peaks in the Franconia Range: Lafayette (behind the hiker), Lincoln, Little Haystack, and Liberty. A magnet for sightseers since the early 1800s, the notch has also become a landmark of the conservation struggle. When logging threatened in the 1920s, the Society for the Protection of New Hampshire Forests roused the nation; schoolchildren, who knew it only through Hawthorne's story "The Great Stone Face," joined the campaign to "Buy a Tree—Save the Notch." The effort succeeded. More recently, Interstate 93 bore down on the narrow pass. Conservationists fought it off until compromise won. The four-lane highway slims down to a two-lane parkway in the notch. New facilities accommodate visitors, who come to share New Hampshire's pleasure in its "sightly places."

ALONG MIDWESTERN

BYROADS

By Dixie Franklin
Photographs by Annie Griffiths

89

W inds that never seem to stop blow fresh across Prairie State Park, kicking up loose sand along the meadows and draws 30 miles north of Joplin, Missouri. Out to explore midwestern parks, I drove toward this sanctuary as its naturalist had advised: "car windows down with the wind blowing free and the smells of spring rushing in." Low hills rolled toward the horizon, broken occasionally by lines of trees along stingy streams. A country lane led me to the park.

"This is a window into presettlement times," said naturalist and administrator Lorence (Larry) Larson. "Prairie once stretched from the Rockies into Ohio in three north-south corridors—tallgrass in the east, shortgrass in the west, mixed species in between."

In 1979, Missouri reached out to preserve this pocket of wind and six-foot tallgrass where Osage Indians once roamed—a remnant of grasses that once grew taller than a man on horseback, that covered 400,000 square miles of North America. The park has 300 species of grasses and wildflowers dominated by bluestem, Indian grass, switch grass, and slough grass. Tucked inside its boundaries are three hiking trails, a picnic area, and the 240-acre Regal Prairie Natural Area. All but 500 acres of the park had escaped the plow, explained Larry, who speaks protectively about overgrazed and tree-encroached land. Careful stewardship is bringing it back to near-presettlement condition.

Prairies, often referred to as seas of grass, are more than oceans of undulating shades of brown to Larry Larson.

"When you're on the prairie, you're in the middle of history," he told me. "Close your eyes and become part of it. Feel the wind, the sun ducking behind the clouds with nothing else around you but prairie smells and sounds. Stop in one of the draws and watch everything disappear except grasses, flowers, and wildlife."

Larry's wife, Hendra, feels it too: "It is not so much what you see. It's what you feel. What you hear."

I listened, trying to "become." Alone, I pitched my tent under a hawthorn tree in a primitive camping area beyond the wash where Fleck Creek gurgles over hard shale and sandstone. I wakened at dawn to the coo and trill of prairie chickens drumming on the lek. Twenty minutes later, the meadow around me came alive with the struttings of prairie chickens in full ceremony. The air was filled with "oo-a-oo" twitterings like vibrations of taut wires in the wind. A young cock strutted about uttering scandalous love talk to one hen after another, whooping it up for the ladies.

I hiked the trails before breakfast, catching a buck and a doe at water's edge. I perched on a turnstile while the bull bison that fancied

Prairie State Park

MISSOURI: NEAR JOPLIN
2,560 ACRES

Indian paintbrush, a flower abundant in spring at Prairie State Park, captures the attention of 10-year-old Erin Larson, a naturalist's daughter.
PRECEDING PAGES: *At the Regal Prairie Natural Area, clouds roil above rare tallgrass prairie, one of the environments preserved in midwest parks.*

himself sultan of his small herd stood leering at me through the electric fence near his sand wallow.

One lazy afternoon I rested under my hawthorn, lounging so still that a bank swallow hopped down beside me all atwitter. Mesmerized, I waited. She hopped up on my head and proceeded to extract strands of hair for refurbishing her nest.

That night, after a brief rain shower with more scowl than force, I thrilled to the wail of coyotes just beyond the stream and giggled when Mike, the German shepherd at the Clovis farm, answered coyote soprano with his authoritative bass.

Soon I, too, felt the prairie that Larry Larson described. Prairie is a private matter. Delicate, yet strong. Friendly, while remaining aloof, a sometimes lonely and hostile place.

"Even the Ozarks were settled before this part of Missouri," Larry told me. "I think part of the reason is that we somehow feel more comfortable among trees and houses."

Now most of the park's visitors, about a thousand a month, come from a 150-mile radius to enjoy the prairie and its animal community. This includes 23 mammal species, 10 fishes, 12 amphibians, 23 reptiles, 144 birds, and 88 butterflies and moths. Crayfish and opossum. Prairie voles and bobcats. Ground squirrels and skunks, chorus frogs and regal fritillary butterflies.

"Native grassland is good for small wildlife. The ground shows bare between grasses. Snakes and birds and other animals can run at ground level like we run between trees. A tumult of life is in the grass," says Larry. I heard him leading a class of third graders on a wildflower hunt: "Wildflowers don't need us to grow, but they need us to enjoy."

The state's former director of parks, John Karel of Columbia, told me that its native prairie was almost lost before this section was saved through the assistance of the Missouri Nature Conservancy. "Given the fact that this state was once one-third prairie and all our sizable parks were in the woods," said John, "the gap in the park system was this big ocean of grass that our ancestors moved across." And only 75,000 scattered acres of Missouri's virgin prairie were left when focus turned to the rocky tract near Joplin. "It is not quite so fertile, and that was its salvation."

I have known men and women dedicated to the preservation of a heritage. Frank Matthews, Sr., of Negaunee, Michigan, spent most of a lifetime collecting relics of the Upper Peninsula's iron industry. His only claim to fame was housed in a lean-to museum and scattered about his yard. Relentlessly, the old man with the flowing white beard hounded politicians. Finally, a few months before he died in 1986, Frank realized his dream: the Michigan Iron Industry Museum and park, on the site of the state's first iron forge, and featuring his collection.

History credits Peter Norbeck with helping to establish Custer State Park in South Dakota. A plaque on Minnesota's North Shore honors Judge C. R. Magney for his efforts to preserve miles of Lake Superior shoreline for future generations. State parks, Magney said, are "every man's country estate."

In Missouri, Larry Larson saves prairie—a hillside at a time, a patch of wildflowers at a time, and sometimes a single sprig of grass.

Dale Slater, a park volunteer, loosened his fist and trailed small red and blue kernels of Indian corn into my palm as the sun warmed the spring morning. I knelt in the roughly plowed garden, dug holes in the hard clay, dropped in the seeds. After traveling midwestern state parks from prairies to pinnacles, I returned once again to New Salem, Illinois. With July sun blasting temperatures almost to 100 degrees, my maize had grown a respectable shoulder high.

Lincoln's New Salem State Historic Site

ILLINOIS: NEAR SPRINGFIELD
700 ACRES

Planting corn in Robert Johnston's garden would probably not have interested young Abraham Lincoln a whit during his years at New Salem, from 1831 to 1837, but it was important to me. Helping a park volunteer was my contribution to a community which had helped to form the ideas and ideals of our 16th President.

Half a million people annually seek out Lincoln's New Salem State Historic Site, on a bluff above the milk-chocolate Sangamon River 20 miles northwest of Springfield. Elderly women in straw sun hats. Teenagers holding hands. A dark-haired matron from the Far East, shimmering sari whipped by a hot summer breeze. Black faces, white faces, tanned, oval, round faces of children peering wide-eyed at the glowing forge as blacksmith Jim Patton pumps the bellows.

"We have people from places you almost never heard of," said park interpreter Lavada Smith.

They come to stroll the streets of hard-packed earth, explore the chinked log cabins, listen to the ping of hammer against anvil at the blacksmith shop, smell the dutch-oven apple pie baking on the hearth at the Rutledge Tavern. They come to sit on the rough benches of Mentor Graham's schoolhouse, smell the herbs in Dr. Francis Regnier's garden, and purchase beeswax and other old-fashioned gifts from the first Berry-Lincoln store. They come for the clomp of horses' hooves, the baa of sheep and gobble of turkeys. But mostly, they come in search of Lincoln.

This is where Lincoln tried shopkeeping, became a surveyor, went to war (against Chief Black Hawk of the Sauk tribe), sampled politics, and left for the state legislature. Other villagers moved on, and New Salem crumbled. The first of its 700 acres were acquired by the state in 1919, but little restoration took place until the 1930s. Since July 1985, this has been a state historic site administered by the Illinois Historic Preservation Agency.

Now Lincoln's New Salem village consists of 23 buildings: log cabins, shops, mills, a tavern and a school, rebuilt as close to original sites as possible. The park includes a museum, campground, picnic area, outdoor theater, and the Talisman River Boat on the muddy Sangamon. But most of all, New Salem is a feeling.

Superintendent David Hedrick and I found the Whalens resting on a bench near the Rutledge Tavern. "Thomas W. and Lois S.," Mr. Whalen emphasized formally. He is a retired druggist from Petersburg, two miles north. With his wife, he walks the village streets daily, "weather permitting." Despite the thousands who visit here, Mr. Whalen told me, it is not a hurry-up place.

I met Harry and Helen Reganti of Rockford, admiring the weathered fences. Marilyn and Howard Witt of Barrington, showing their Yugoslavian cousins a bit of American history and being surprised at what they already knew; six-year-old Laura Witt wondering why there were no toys in the cabins, four-year-old Ashley whining for an ice cream cone.

Marlene Cantrill was here with her family from Australia, touring Illinois after missionary training in LaGrange. Back home, Marlene had read about Lincoln. Suddenly, choking back her emotions, she wrapped her arms about her young daughter Sara. "We read one story and we cried and cried," she said. "It was about the boy who was to be shot and his sister begged the President to save him." That was 18-year-old William Scott of Company K, Third Vermont, who fell asleep on sentry duty in September 1861. Lincoln spared his life.

At the museum, Barbara Lengiewicz, now of Springfield, explained gristmill artifacts to her mother, a visitor from Warsaw, Poland. "Your history is only 200 years old. Ours is more like 1,000," Barbara remarked to me.

The park can be a relaxing hour, a lesson in pioneer life, an interlude in a lifelong study of Lincoln. Nowhere in New Salem is he more real than in the three Great American People Shows, by John Ahart, which have played here every summer since 1976, stylized portrayals of the life of Lincoln and his continuing effect on America. Moved by the performance I saw one evening, I felt the sameness of things Lincoln must have known: the fireflies, the stars, and finally the cicadas that rasped on and on and on.

Most of New Salem's visitors also seek out Lincoln attractions in Springfield: the home, supervised by the National Park Service; the law office; the Old State Capitol; and the Lincoln Tomb. In the early days, an official told me at the capitol, Lincoln and other legislators would climb the dome to gaze out over the prairie. Did he remember that view in the 1860s, I wonder, when he was leading the war to save the Union?

Fort Robinson State Park

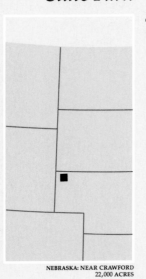

At Fort Robinson, in Nebraska, the people rose in defense when its future was in doubt, helping to bring 22,000 acres into a state park through a campaign that began in 1955. "It was such a part of the area that the people did not want to let it go," says Tom Buecker, curator of its museum. This park in the Pine Ridge country has a checkered past: a U.S. Department of Agriculture station; the world's largest Quartermaster Remount Depot; Olympic equestrian training grounds; War Dog Reception and Training Corps with 1,600 kennels; artillery training area with the pockmarks of shellbursts still visible on the buttes. The last gathering point of the great Sioux Nation lies a stone's throw from a prisoner-of-war camp for German soldiers.

Nearby, in 1873, the Red Cloud Indian Agency was built to issue government rations and annuities to the 13,000 Oglala Sioux, Cheyenne, and other Sioux tribes encamped along the White River. In 1874, the fort's first 949 soldiers marched in to protect the agency from possible hostilities. White prospectors were invading Sioux territory, and war flared through the region. Here, precarious Dull Knife Pass marks the route where Dull Knife's small band escaped in the daring, futile run for freedom called the Cheyenne Outbreak. Chief Crazy

Horse died at the fort from a bayonet wound when he came in to surrender in 1877. And the post saw service from the Army's Ninth and Tenth Cavalry Regiments, crack units with white officers and black enlisted men—called "Buffalo Soldiers" by the Indians because curly hair reminded them of the hair of buffalo. Today, both Fort Robinson and the Red Cloud Agency are Registered National Historic Landmarks.

Of the original 330 buildings, about 60 are maintained through the cooperation of three Nebraska agencies: the Game and Parks Commission; the State Historical Society, which directs a museum focused on the opening of the plains for settlement; and the University of Nebraska, which maintains the Trailside Museum of natural history. Chadron State College manages the post playhouse.

"This is a family-oriented park which everyone in Nebraska can afford," says Superintendent Vince Rotherham. "Every time you change directions, you get a different view."

A hundred miles long, the Pine Ridge of northwest Nebraska is an extension of both the Badlands and the Black Hills of South Dakota. Its 500-foot buttes are stark white in the noonday sun, tempered to smoky gray with evening shadows, fiery pink in the path of a sudden storm. Ponderosa pines on the summits smell like vanilla and butterscotch, in air tinged with the burning dryness of sun on rocks. It's easy, as Vince Rotherham says, "to imagine an Indian behind every butte."

Valleys were green from recent rains when I rounded Saddle Rock Butte just north of Crawford. Yucca, the pioneers' soap weed, dominated the slopes. There's a story about a local rancher's daughter whose formal wedding flowers failed to arrive in time. As in a good western movie, the day was saved when ranch hands went out and picked armfuls of ivory yucca blossoms to decorate the ranch house and the wedding chapel.

I arrived at the enlisted men's barracks, now the park's main lodge, in time for a buffalo lunch. I do believe this park can outdo Custer State Park's buffalo menu, although Custer has about six times the herd. At Fort Robinson I ate buffalo steak, stew, hot dogs, hamburgers, pizza—buffalo in almost every form. (Not until Blue Bell Lodge at Custer, however, was I served buffalo steak for breakfast, with scrambled eggs and toast.)

Fort Robinson offers such a wide choice of activities to its visitors—350,000 of them a year—that a line begins to form at the sign-up booth before 7 a.m. I didn't want to miss anything: Touring the museums. Driving in an open jeep through the herd of 250 buffalo. Fishing Soldier Creek for trout with Walt Meckem, who grew up among these ridges. Singing around the evening campfire after a chuckwagon cookout of more buffalo stew and cornbread. A creaky hay-wagon ride to the playhouse to hiss and boo and cheer at the nightly melodrama.

After dark, lights from the 1909-style lampposts cast soft halos on the old parade grounds. I imagined the cadence of marching soldiers, and of horses leaping the stiles that occupied the parade grounds during remount days.

Almost all the army mules and horses in the entire west were requisitioned from Fort Robinson. As many as 17,000 at a time were quartered here. At a post reunion and elsewhere, I met veterans who remembered that era. Brig. Gen. J. Andrew Seitz (Ret.), former post commander of Fort Riley, Kansas, said those were still the days "when we were animal-oriented people, a time where horse outfits were lean and mean. There was a confidence about them. They wore spurs that clinked, and carried themselves with a different air."

"We burned up in the summer and froze in the winter," said William (Arky) Watts of Gulfport, Mississippi, who came out of the back hills of Arkansas to enlist. "I knew mules, but not horses. There was nothing in that bunch but cowboys, sheepherders, and me."

Arky was stationed here with the 698th Quartermaster Remount Troop from 1939 to 1943, and was hoping to complete his search for the 58 men of his outfit. He could account for all but six. The unit had left with a detail of pack mules bound for Burma.

Horses and mules still fill an important role around here, with rodeos a highlight of most festivals and fairs. A sign at the Sno-White Laundromat in Crawford warns: "No Horse or Saddle Blankets. Thank You."

When I rode out in the Fort Robinson stagecoach, driver Ralph Staman shifted his hand-rolled cigarette between his lips and said he has worked horses "as long as I am alive, as many years as I am old." With his sweat-stained felt hat, his heavy stomp on the stage apron to get his mules on the go, Ralph has become the hero of five-year-old Michael, son of Tom Buecker. When we came in, Michael relinquished the end of the reins, climbed down from between us on the stage seat, and boasted, "I helped Ralph drive."

I went out alone to the site of the Red Cloud agency, standing on a knoll with hot Nebraska wind scorching my face, seeing—as Tom Buecker sees—hundreds of Indian tipis along the stream.

I hiked through the blossoming yucca and up McKenzie Pass, walking the wagon ruts cut by supply trains a hundred years ago. I felt the heat of Toadstool Park, north of Fort Robinson, where the terrain suddenly turns barren with stark sandstone mushrooms and grotesque formations sculpted by the wind.

One Sunday morning, I went out with Grace and Alan Wilwand, who live nearby. We followed a precarious wildlife trail up a thousand-foot butte overlooking an immense plain. At the top, protected by outcroppings, were seven signal-fire rings; double rings faced the Black Hills and the Badlands, and one huge fire ring faced Fort Robinson. Scattered under a toppled pine were chips of jasper where forgotten warriors had perfected their weapons while on watch. Below me, a thin line still marked an ancient buffalo trail across ranchers' grazing land. I had spotted a pioneer cabin, almost hidden by ponderosa down a dim canyon, and while I pondered life as it must have been there, the reverberating cry of a lone coyote echoed up the cliffs.

These ridges hold many legends, many roots, and have attracted many painters. An artists' favorite is legendary Crow Butte, which protrudes like a fortress above the flatlands southwest of Crawford. A Crow band made this butte an escape route after their attack on James Bordeaux's fur trading post east of Chadron. Abandoned in 1876, the post was reconstructed in 1956 for the Museum of the Fur Trade, which attracts almost 50,000 visitors a year.

Τhe Great Lakes also figured in the fur trade as voyageurs searched for new routes to the west. Lake Superior's North Shore now draws visitors to the six Minnesota parks that a state official has called "a string of diamonds on the shoulder of the Midwest." About 650,000 people annually follow U.S. 61 northeast from Duluth to Gooseberry Falls, Split Rock Lighthouse, Tettegouche, Temperance River, Cascade River, and Judge Magney.

Manager Paul Sundberg of Gooseberry Falls says they come primarily to experience the "uniqueness of so many streams that cascade into Lake Superior," and to see this greatest of the Great Lakes in all its changing moods, "the roar and power of the water."

Lake Superior is the Midwest's ocean, Hiawatha's Big Sea Water, a lake too wide to see across, an inland sea with cliffs and sandy coves, waves and storms, and tide-like seiches. It is a sea without the smell of sea, a sea as fresh as a morning shower. Visitors walk her shores to refresh the spirit.

The parks are where people from the Twin Cities of Minneapolis and St. Paul come to escape from summer heat, to prowl the shoreline, search for agates; to fish, sail, camp, and hike. Only the hardiest swim more than big-toe deep, as lake temperature seldom comes within 40 degrees of body temperature even on the hottest days. In winter, some return to ski the cross-country trails.

"I'm glad there are places like this. It makes people civilized again," said Sharon Brovold of Minneapolis as she pitched her tent near the Gooseberry River. Each park claims its own tannin-stained river, complete with foam. Each river carves its own way to Superior, lingering in reflective pools, squeezing through gorges and thunking in its potholes before roaring off to grand-finale falls.

As the first gem in this necklace of parks, Gooseberry Falls has visitors every day from mid-May through the October color season, enjoying its stairstep waterfalls and scenic hiking trails.

Split Rock Lighthouse State Park is a joint venture of the Division of Parks and Recreation and the Minnesota Historical Society, which manages the 1910 light station and living history center. For almost 60 years, the light and the two-toned *Beee-oooh* fog signal guided ships to Two Harbors and Duluth to take on grain and iron ore.

Established in 1979, Tettegouche at Baptism River is the newest of the six. I followed its Lake Superior trail along Shovel Point through a forest that grew smaller as the underlying rock bared itself to the elements. I paused at overlooks to gaze at cozy coves, towering cliffs, and the Palisades, which have become Minnesota's most photographed natural shoreline landmark. Staring at the 170-foot cliffs, I marveled at the rock climbers who rappel down to the water and climb back up again.

Farther along the shore, I hiked the trail beside Temperance River with park manager Allan Barry. He told me that before swimming was prohibited in these parks for safety's sake, divers would leap from 60-foot cliffs into the pools below the waterfalls. "When girls dived," he remarked, "it almost took their tops off."

Allan's father, Bob, manages Cascade River State Park, where the namesake stream glides over low lava shelves like maple syrup, its white foam like lace on a bridal gown. After the tumult of other North Shore rivers, Cascade is a drama in slow motion.

*Lake Superior's
North Shore
State Parks*

MINNESOTA: GOOSEBERRY FALLS,
SPLIT ROCK LIGHTHOUSE, TETTEGOUCHE,
TEMPERANCE RIVER, CASCADE RIVER,
JUDGE C.R. MAGNEY; NEAR DULUTH
TOTAL ACREAGE 15,685

Even if I had tired of waterfalls by the time I reached Judge Magney, the Devil's Kettle would have taken me by surprise. A midstream boulder splits Brule River into twin falls. Both come thundering down—and the southern half of the river simply disappears. Manager Tom Ludwig says no one can be sure if, or where, the vanished river surfaces again.

Surrounded by outdoor splendor, I could not resist the campgrounds. I pitched my tent among friendly folks. At night, I listened to the thump of ax against campfire log, the snap of kindling; crickets; crackle and sizzle of campfires; a ripple of laughter; and finally only the swish of water on rocks. Sounds of contentment!

"Campers are interesting people because they're out doing what they want to do," says volunteer campground hostess Beflyn Pruden, at Gooseberry Falls. She has been coming to these parks for more than 30 summers. Nursing a sore wrist from a fall on a muddy trail, she said the accident was almost worth it. Jim Hiller of Le Roy, age 12, took her arm to make sure she didn't fall again, and showed up later with his brother Paul to split her campfire wood.

"Here," says Tom Bothwell from Wheeler, "we can reach out and grab so many experiences." Like those of the nine-year-old who earned points toward a junior park naturalist's badge by counting noses on a geology hike. Or those treasured by Roy and Mary Boyden of St. Paul, who brought their grandchildren along: "When we were parents, we didn't have time to do these things."

Or those in the tales of voyageurs, old-time Norwegian fishermen like Rangvold Sve and Helmer Aakvik, lumbermen, miners, sailors; of early pioneers who lived on salt herring and venison and modern pioneers who prefer hot dogs on a stick and s'mores oozing with marshmallows roasted over a smoky campfire. Sweater nights and idyllic days. A loon calling at twilight. Chipmunks noseying around my tent. Deer. Peregrine falcons being reintroduced to the crags and crannies of the cliffs. Moose that "attacked" a frontyard lilac bush at Cascade River. The North Shore is fog, sunshine, rushing water, with summer's heat inland beyond the Sawtooth Mountains and winter in the offing.

"Lake Superior is so smooth at times that I can take a canoe out, and then in October and November it wouldn't be safe out there in a battleship," says Richard Hoskins, assistant manager at Cascade River. Paul Sundberg says these storms "pick up beach and put it down again with sounds that are hard to describe." Lee Radzak, manager of the historic site at Split Rock Lighthouse, says that at times "waves come sweeping across the lake to climb the 130-foot cliffs and coat the lighthouse with ice."

Helmer Aakvik, who was past 90 when he died in January 1987, wrenched a living from the lake for years. He agreed that it can be "bad enough." In 1958 he won a Carnegie medal of heroism for an unsuccessful attempt to rescue a neighbor caught in a storm. For 29 hours, with temperatures near zero, he battled 23-foot waves in a flat-bottomed fishing boat. "I was a busy man," he told me in a soft, firm voice with a clipped Norwegian accent. "I didn't even have time to pray, but I didn't expect an angel to come and pick me up and take me to shore anyway." He loved the lake with all its fury because spring always comes again.

Devil's Lake State Park

pring was green in the Wisconsin forest and ice was far from my mind when I drove through the tunnel of trees at the entrance of Devil's Lake State Park. Fern fronds unfurled along the roadside, waving invitingly. The flowers of May blossomed as colorful as an untamed country garden on the forest floor and among the rock outcroppings.

Then I spotted it through the trees, a sapphire lake cupped in the hollow of 500-foot quartzite bluffs, chimneys, outcroppings, and spilled talus boulders. Soft rain draped mist across the valley, diffusing the light and intensifying the colors. I was looking at the playground of southern Wisconsin and Chicago.

WISCONSIN: NEAR BARABOO
8,600 ACRES

"The whole park has been the front yard of Wisconsin for two, three, and four generations," says Ralph Tuttle, now retired after serving here for 46 years. Rocks and water, climbing and camping, picnicking and wildflower-watching attract 1.25 million people a year—along with swimming, fishing, scuba diving, hiking, and seeking out the effigy mounds built by Native Americans about a thousand years ago.

In 1971 the park became part of an Ice Age National Scientific Reserve, and the lovely ravine called Parfrey's Glen has special status as a "Scientific Area," but Devil's Lake has been an outdoor geology lab for many years. A glacier diverted an ancient river here, and plugged the river gorge at two spots with morainal debris, creating the lake. Ice also covered the eastern half of the high ground surrounding the lake, the canoe-shaped enclosure called the Baraboo Hills.

From clifftop, the valley seems dwarfed: doll-size picnickers, toy fishing boats, a miniature train chugging along shoreline tracks. A black-and-yellow bee bumbles its way through the wild sweet peas; small brown grasshoppers pop like popcorn ahead of hiking shoes. It is from these ridges that one can almost reach out to wring intense color from the sky, the forest, and the flowers. Blue of the sky seems to dribble into the lake, baby blue in the shadows.

On the Tumbled Rocks Trail at the bottom of the bluffs, talus which seems dull at a distance is dappled with color. Mauve. Orange. Pink. Reddish hues of iron oxide make patterns on boulders overlaid with grayish lichen.

Many visitors come with a dual purpose, says Administrator Wayne Schutte: They visit the park, then tour nearby attractions. These include the scenic waterways of the Wisconsin Dells, and the Circus World Museum at Baraboo. For a while, Wayne offered Circus World discount coupons to every child who filled a garbage bag with litter. The park was cleaner than it had been in years—and then "a few kids got wise and found the dumpsters."

One morning in Baraboo, I found four members of the Chicago Mountaineering Club drinking orange juice and coffee, waiting for the park bluffs to dry from early mist. Throughout the Midwest, club members like these learn alpine-style climbing at Devil's Lake.

Julie Krumpen of Ann Arbor, Michigan, travels for nine hours most weekends to climb with the Chicago group. She is disappointed if the rocks "turn greasy when it rains—except that I like the area so much I come anyway." "On a nice day," said Bob Demkowicz, "climbers are all over the cliffs like ants." They learn on these bluffs, he told me, and go on to climb throughout the world.

Custer State Park

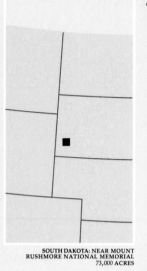

SOUTH DAKOTA: NEAR MOUNT
RUSHMORE NATIONAL MEMORIAL
73,000 ACRES

Devil's Lake was my preparation for here," said climber Neal McDermott of Arlington Heights, Illinois. He had just finished a difficult route in the aptly named Needles of South Dakota's Custer State Park. His companion, Jill Bjorndahl of Chicago, agreed. She pointed to the spires: "These are so small on top. When I get to the top at Devil's Lake, I can run for a mile."

I had been watching the climbers with Jan and Herb Conn, who pioneered climbing in the Needles. They began in 1947, and made first ascents of more than 200 peaks before they switched to caving. Herb also did what few climbers have been allowed—he looked George Washington straight in the eye. From 1962 to 1975, he maintained the great carved faces at Mount Rushmore. I joined this unassuming couple for a front-porch picnic at the home they built in a valley bordering Custer State Park. They prefer the quiet life, Jan told me: They get water from rainbarrels, or they melt snow; they do without electricity; they haven't eaten in a restaurant for 30 years.

Of the park's visitors, almost a million a year, many take a more hectic pace. They linger here a few days on their way to or from Mount Rushmore National Memorial, the Crazy Horse Memorial nearby, or Yellowstone National Park. They can sample leisure at Custer's campgrounds or its four resorts, and watch demonstrations of panning for Black Hills gold, discovered by Gen. George A. Custer's expedition in 1874.

Even Custer's expedition was astonished by the wildflowers. Old accounts tell of flowers so tall that cavalrymen reached from the saddle to scoop up large bouquets as they rode into the French Creek valley, where a re-created stockade stands today. There I watched park staff members burn flapjacks over an open fire, as the first white settlers must have done in 1874 when they sneaked into the Black Hills. Those settlers were breaking the terms of a federal treaty with the Sioux; the Indians' anger fed the war in which Custer was killed.

The sacred hills were called Paha Sapa by the Sioux, which might be rendered as "Land of Shadows" in Sioux myths. Shadows mark the lush green treeline which appears black in the shadowy distance, giving the Black Hills their current name. Shadows dance along the rippling streams, the artificial lakes, the ridges dominated by singing ponderosa pines. Visitors say the butterscotch scent of the trees can be detected for miles across the hot summer plains.

Designated a state game preserve in 1913, the area became a state park six years later, largely through the efforts of Governor Peter Norbeck. My admiration for Norbeck grew as I negotiated the 14 miles of Needles Highway Scenic Drive. He had laid it out on foot and horseback, with hairpin turns along sheer cliffs and S-curves around granite spires to provide optimum views. Nobody had to warn me to take it slow. As the park's director Rollie Noem says, "People come expecting hills and find mountains."

On the Iron Mountain Road, which begins in the park, I stopped at every tunnel and overlook to savor the approaching faces of Mount Rushmore. I was no less fascinated by the roads and bridges that twist like a pig's tail through and across canyons. But it was the park's 18-mile Wildlife Loop Road that stole much of my time. Here wildlife runs free: elk, mule deer and whitetails, pronghorns, coyotes.

100

One morning I set out to find the buffalo with Katherine Murdock, whose ranch is only an hour's drive away. We rounded a sandstone outcropping on the Loop Road and there they were! They filled the valley 500 strong, haughtily stopping traffic for a quarter of a mile. "They could be cowboys in their furry chaps," said Katherine.

Custer has all the outdoor attractions—camping and hiking, swimming and fishing and horseback riding—but most visitors come to see the buffalo. I watched calves bouncing around like stiff-legged rocking horses in red-brown coats. One veered from the herd of stoic elders to scatter a flock of cowbirds.

Fred Matthews told me he has seen 2,000-pound animals in a romping mood, playing follow-the-leader. He has worked with the herd at Custer since 1955, starting as a buffalo skinner. "As big as they are, you'd think they were so bundlesome you wouldn't have to worry about gettin' away from them," he drawled, "but they're just the opposite." The park controls herd size by a sale of surplus animals and a limited hunting season, after a roundup that Fred supervises every fall. This involves horseback, jeep, and helicopter units, and it "can get wild and woolly," he said with a grin.

As part of the state's Junior Ranger program, naturalists teach youngsters to respect the buffalo and all of nature. I tagged along with staffer Susan Hirschy and 13 youngsters on a nature hike.

"Don't touch the three leaves because it will make you itch and make you feel like you're gonna die," warned Stephen Prested of Berkley, Michigan. He was under-age for the hike, but who could refuse a tousle-haired four-year-old still wearing his breakfast chocolate mustache?

After leap-frogging a stream on convenient rocks and leading a walk through the forest, Susan organized a "Snake-in-the-Grass" hide-and-seek game. "I've got buffalo chips on my head," whined a child from his tallgrass hiding place. "Get down," Susan told him firmly. "This is a wilderness experience."

To Bob and Della Dahlgren of Minneapolis, the wilderness is buffalo meandering across the lodge lawns and deer on the roads. For John Madden of Ocean Springs, Mississippi, it's going to sleep to the music of the creek spilling over the dam. For me, Custer is coolness of the nights, sudden erratic storms followed by filtered sunlight, fishing French Creek Natural Area alone, and meeting burros on the North Road that felt no shame at begging and scrounging my last cookie.

I found loyalty in all the midwestern state parks, but nowhere was loyalty more intense than at Custer. As naturalist Sally Goebel says, Custer and the Black Hills are home for a lot of people "whether they live here or not."

Tim Clarke felt the appeal of the Black Hills many miles away. He grew up in Rapid City, then went to war. "In Vietnam, I would be hot and sweaty. I could cool myself off by thinking of the Black Hills," Tim said. "I could look at the moon and be OK, knowing it was the same moon that was shining on the Black Hills."

When it was time to leave, I headed east with the Black Hills over my shoulder. I checked my rear-view mirror all the way until they were only a dark shadow along the horizon—Paha Sapa. Was there a hint of butterscotch in the air?

Prairie
State Park

With jumps as high as 18 inches,
a greater prairie chicken performs a
ritual of early springtime
courtship. Shortly after sunrise,
a visitor may see dozens of males
gathering at their booming grounds,
named for their singular nuptial
call. It resembles the sound
produced by blowing across the top
of an empty bottle, and can carry a
mile or so across the prairie. For
several weeks the females remain
aloof, waiting until mid-April to
choose a mate. A hen lays a clutch
of 10 to 14 eggs and incubates them
for 23 days; the chicks can leave
the nest within 24 hours. Above
left, a female red-winged blackbird
perches on a cattail; only the male
has the flashy red shoulder patch
that inspired the common name.
More than 300 species of grasses
and wildflowers flourish in Prairie
State Park. This habitat supports
a wide range of wildlife. Besides
more than 140 bird species found
here, mammals ranging from the
least shrew to the wary coyote
and the mighty American bison
make their homes in the park.

Prairie fire! Once a cry that filled
homesteaders' hearts with dread,
the phrase now denotes a technique
for managing prairie lands. Here
workers set the grasses ablaze with
drip torches after carefully analyzing
wind, weather, the moisture content
of the plants, and other factors.
Controlled burning kills unwanted
invaders such as thorny shrubs
and persimmon saplings, and hastens
the return of minerals to the soil.
The blackened surface will soon turn
green with shoots of fire-tolerant
prairie grasses and flowers.

Lincoln's New Salem State Historic Site

August afternoon draws young fishermen to the banks of the Sangamon River. As aimless as they, 22-year-old Abraham Lincoln settled here in 1831. An ox-drawn Conestoga (below) recalls a story he told years later. While a shopkeeper here—not a very diligent or successful one—Lincoln bought a barrel from a westbound pioneer; in it, he found a lawbook: "The more I read, the more intensely interested I became. . . ." By the time he moved to Springfield in 1837, he had embarked on the paths of law and politics that would lead to the White House. At right, a youthful scholar rests his slate and lunch basket on a rough-hewn New Salem windowsill.

Fort Robinson
State Park

With jingle of harness and creak
of wheel, mules Sandy and Sam
pull a replica of the Sidney-
Deadwood stagecoach near the old
buildings at Fort Robinson State
Park. Often children share the
driver's seat and even hold the end
of the reins. The short trip, which
includes a splashing ford of
Soldier's Creek, helps visitors savor
the atmosphere of a century ago.
Established in 1874 as Camp
Robinson to quell Indian uprisings
and to protect the nearby Red
Cloud Indian Agency, the post
served in the 1940s as a training
center supplying dogs for K-9 units
and as a POW camp for captured
German soldiers. As late as
World War II it supplied mules
for active duty overseas. Driver
Ralph Staman (left) wears a
yellow neckerchief, color of cavalry
emblems, recalling the early 1920s
and '30s when the post bred and
trained horses for cavalry units—
its fox hunts (for coyotes) and polo
teams made it famous as "the
country club of the Army."

FOLLOWING PAGES: Prairie
panorama greets park employees
dressed up as 19th-century
cavalrymen. The 4,900-foot-high
Red Cloud Buttes overlooking
Fort Robinson mark the southern
boundary of the badlands
of South Dakota and Nebraska.

Lake Superior's North Shore State Parks

Staunch silhouette of Split Rock Lighthouse, commissioned in 1910, overlooks Lake Superior. Its ten-second beacon and its foghorn served shipping for more than half a century. The barely accessible location required that supplies—and visitors—ride a platform hoisted by a steam-powered derrick until engineers built a tramway in 1916. Eight years later the North Shore highway opened the region to motorists. Today, a chain of six state parks lures visitors to the rugged cliffs, sandy coves, and sparkling waterfalls along the shore of Superior.

Dip of a paddle ripples the surface of Lake Superior as canoeists take an early morning cruise off Cascade River. Experienced boaters stay close to land, for storms can churn up raging waves in minutes. "We lost 36 automobiles from our weather deck," wrote one ferry captain after a 1940 storm,

". . . and counted ourselves lucky not to lose the ship itself."

FOLLOWING PAGES: *At summer's height, roadside lupines brighten U.S. Route 61, the North Shore highway, somewhere between Gooseberry Falls and Tettegouche State Parks.*

Devil's Lake
State Park

Baraboo Hills (above) roll toward the horizon beyond Devil's Lake, known to the Winnebago Indians as Spirit Lake. They established summer camps on its shores and canoed its sapphire waters, fishing with bone hooks for perch, sunfish, bass, pike, and other species. Today's visitors—as many as 3,000 on a busy day—crowd the north shore beach (left), swimming, sailboarding, fishing, and soaking up the sun of an August afternoon. Established in 1900, Wisconsin's park system claims at least one state park within an hour's drive of every resident of the state. This includes 58 parks, 4 recreational forests, 3 recreational areas, and 11 state trails created from abandoned railroad right-of-way. With tracks and ties removed and a crushed-limestone surface in place, these trails offer about 340 almost level miles for hikers and bikers— or snowmobilers in winter.

Custer
State Park

Bison graze the Black Hills
of South Dakota, part of one
of the largest publicly owned herds
in the United States. In summer,
these 1,400 or so animals divide
into several shifting herds. Below,
a protective cow keeps watch as her
calf nuzzles for milk. Adult bison
here may weigh 1,500 pounds and
can run as fast as 35 miles an hour;
park officials warn visitors to
stay at a safe distance.

FOLLOWING PAGES: Ponderosa
pine stands sentinel at prairie's
edge near the park's southern
boundary. Largest midwest state
park, Custer's 73,000 acres vary
from rolling hills to rocky spires.

OUT IN THE HIGH

COUNTRY

By Thomas B. Allen
Photographs by Thomas Nebbia

Asmall gray bird suddenly plunged into the white water tumbling down the mountain ravine. A moment later it emerged, an insect clutched in its beak. It skimmed over the froth and landed on a water-slick rock directly across from where we sat. At that instant, three tiny pink triangles appeared in a dark, moss-lined crack above the rock. Over the roar of the river we could hear a faint chirping. The gray bird flew up and transferred the insect to one of the triangles, now faintly discernible as the maw of a sharp-beaked little bird. As the harried parent zipped off again over the rapids, its mate flew up to the nest and continued the feeding ritual.

The water dippers' performance took place in July before an audience of two on the Middle Fork of the Popo Agie River at Sinks Canyon State Park, about seven miles southwest of Lander, Wyoming. My wife, Scottie, and I had the river to ourselves, as far as we could see upstream or down.

On another day, we had a canyon wall to ourselves. A storm opened that show with an overture of clouds that cast rippling shadows across the brush-dotted slope. Then sun and shadows disappeared and huge raindrops came, driving us to shelter under the ground-hugging branches of a squat Rocky Mountain juniper. Hailstones pelted the powdery soil, rattling and bouncing off rocks.

The storm passed as swiftly as it had come, and we continued along the slope, enjoying the solitude as much as the splendor. We picked our way through scree and sagebrush on a great-circle course that took us up about a thousand feet, across the face of the slope, and gradually down again, a little more than a mile from our starting point. From on high, the Popo Agie looked like a shimmering white thread stitched in the greens and grays of forest and rock.

That night we camped at the riverside. A grove of aspen and the low, ceaseless roar of the tumbling water closed out the sight and the sounds of other campers. You can feel alone here, a few hours' drive from the throngs at Yellowstone and Grand Teton National Parks.

Sinks Canyon, which is smaller than New York City's Central Park, is an oasis for travelers heading toward the national parks. But the principal beneficiaries are local people, who treat Sinks Canyon like their own big backyard. There is a sense of pilgrimage in the way they bring their own visitors to the park. Often the first stop is at The Sinks. Here the Middle Fork of the Popo Agie rounds a sharp bend, cascades over and around a jumble of boulders, enters a large cavern at the base of a cliff—and vanishes. People gather at the jagged mouth of the cavern and gape at what is no longer there.

Then they go about half a mile down the road that follows the

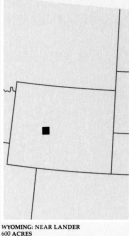

Sinks Canyon State Park

WYOMING: NEAR LANDER
600 ACRES

Announcing spring, the Popo Agie River floods its valley in Wyoming's Sinks Canyon State Park. Wild places—forests, lakes, deserts—of the Rocky Mountain region offer many ways for visitors to enjoy nature's gifts.
PRECEDING PAGES: A mountaineer savors the solitude of Sinks Canyon.

river. At what is called The Rise they walk out onto a wooden platform jutting 25 feet above the spot where a now tranquil Popo Agie reappears. As part of the pilgrimage, they throw down chunks of bread for huge rainbow and brown trout that leap up to snatch a meal. "You can always tell the local people," Superintendent Ron Livesay told me as we stood on the platform. "They bring the bread with them. The out-of-towners see what's going on and run back to their cars to get some food to throw." And only a stranger asks about fishing for the monsters in the pool. The answer: no fishing at The Rise—these fish get special protection.

Crow Indians gave the Popo Agie (pronounced "po-*po*-shia") its name, which probably meant "the beginning of the waters." Ever since the Indians named the river, the belief persisted that the same river disappeared and reappeared. Not until 1983, however, was there a record of proof. Scientists put red dye into the water at The Sinks while colleagues watched for it at The Rise. They had an unexpected two-hour wait. Apparently the swift water slowed down in channels through the limestone that underlies the area, or in some unknown underground lake.

From The Rise, the river flows toward Lander, a friendly old town, between canyon walls of remarkably different character. Winter sun warms the one that faces south, and the snow there melts in response. The meltwater flows away. Because of this loss of precious moisture, little more than sagebrush, grasses, and stunted trees can grow on that slope. Douglas fir, limber pine, and other sturdy trees blanket the slope facing north, where the soil takes up more snowmelt. In fact, the canyon walls differ so much that several of the park's 94 species of birds are normally found on one slope only.

Small as it is, Sinks Canyon contains a respectable number of wildflowers. On the mile-long nature trail, Ron pointed out several, including a pale green bog orchid and sticky purple geraniums. He crushed the leaves of another plant and identified it as horsemint, an Indian medicine. At the riverbank, he watched a red squirrel carrying off a morsel. "Summer in Wyoming," Ron said, "is a time to get ready for winter. For us and them."

The highway through Sinks Canyon turns into a dirt road just south of the park and switchbacks up to the high country of Shoshone National Forest. The Loop Road, as it is known, winds through the forest for 26 miles and ends at a highway near South Pass City, a ghost town restored as a historic site. In winter, the road that we bounded along would be part of a network of snowmobile trails. In midsummer, it took us to a ridge that looks out onto the snow-topped peaks of the Wind River Range. Winter here is never far away: Snow often keeps the Loop Road closed till the end of June.

Our first stop was at a meadow favored by moose. We had to settle for a marmot sunning on a rock. Farther along, we picked up a hitchhiking fisherman from Ohio who returns every year to one of the lakes along the road. "Mostly rainbows," he said, patting his creel. His campsite, a couple of miles along, was deserted. "My wife took the kids into town to buy food," he said. "I think they're getting tired of fish."

After dropping him off we kept climbing, past brooks and glens and stands of pine. In a tract that had been clear-cut years ago, young trees were growing. A flash of color—yellow water lilies—lured us to a little pond. We were at 9,000 feet, near the high point on the road. Yet, surrounded by pines and seclusion, we had no sense of being in the high country.

For that, you need a ridge, even one at a mere 6,000 feet. We found that ridge on a trail that ran across the top of Stillwater State Forest in northwestern Montana. We still had seclusion, but with it the exultation of space, the soaring of freedom.

Wildflowers bordered the trail—fiery Indian paintbrush, purple aster, the white-plumed stalks of beargrass, little bouquets of violet lodgepole lupine, lambstongue, glacier lily, harebell. Farther on, the trail dipped and rose between small, rock-strewn hillocks; patches of white lay ghostlike among shadowy ridges below us.

"I'm going to find some snow," Scottie said. I stayed on the higher ridge, looking at the wildflowers. She was soon out of sight, but I followed her trail along a rocky path by an occasional footprint in July snow. I climbed around a large, lichen-spotted rock and saw her crouched over a few pale purple asters at the edge of a drift. "Look at this," she said, standing up; "I've never seen wildflowers growing in snow." She smiled an Easterner's smile of surprise. "I have one foot in winter and one foot in spring."

Back on the high trail, we flushed a grouse that promptly landed again, near us. On another hillock, a hummingbird hovered over my head as if looking for a flower in my hat. About us wheeled noisy gray birds with black-and-white wings—Clark's nutcrackers, named after their discoverer, the Clark of Lewis and Clark.

The birds gave the ridge a paradisiacal air, a sense that human beings rarely appeared in this high, radiant place. In fact, the high trail—hardly a scratch on the rock—had opened only shortly before. Snow had blocked the trail to Werner Peak until the Fourth of July.

This peak memorializes one Rudolph J. Werner, better known as Joe Bush, whose roguish saga is piquant even for the West. Dishonorably discharged from the U.S. Army for shooting a corporal in an argument, Joe turned to horse-stealing. A leg full of a rancher's buckshot ended that career. In 1887, after a stint of working on the railroad, he homesteaded nearby and became a trapper. When another trapper began to run a line through what Joe said was Joe's valley, Joe burned down the competitor's cabin.

So, in fitting memory, a fire lookout's tower now rises above his peak. Scottie and I had volunteered to serve in place of the regular lookout, Dave Smith, on his day off. Dave's instructions included warnings to stay away from metal during storms. "Don't get between metal objects like the stove and Firefinder," he told us. The Osborne Firefinder, mounted on a platform in the center of the tower, was a sighting device that slid on a rail around a map of the forest. I was also given a quick lesson on how to use the radio to report a fire to the forest headquarters.

I had been a lookout for about three hours when I saw a wisp of

Stillwater State Forest

MONTANA: NEAR GLACIER
NATIONAL PARK
90,000 ACRES

smoke rising from a distant ridge. I swung the Firefinder around the track, lined the sight up with the wisp, tried desperately to read the worn compass bearings engraved on the rim, and switched on the radio. A calm voice responded to my breathless report. A few minutes later, while I tried to remember whether I had called in 143 or 134 as a bearing, I was told that I had seen an authorized fire, a routine brush-burning on a resort's ski run. "Don't feel bad," the kindly voice said. "You done good."

We enjoyed our stay in the tower—the big night sky, the mule deer bathed in moonlight below us. But, amateurs though we were, we had a job to do. A state forest is not a state park. People are expected to enjoy a park. A state forest, at least in Montana, must earn its keep.

Under Montana law, Tom Vars, supervisor of Stillwater's 90,000 acres, must run the forest to make money. Income from timber sales goes to various trust funds devoted to education, and he often mentions "the trusts." But he is a man in love with his forest and he recognizes a stewardship over it that goes beyond making money.

"Recreation is part of what is expected of us. But only a part," Vars told me. "Before we have a timber sale, we have to have the land checked out by the experts. First, is there anything historical, anything of archaeological interest?" He lit his pipe and continued the litany. We were sitting in the log cabin that is his headquarters, itself designated a national historic site. "There are hydrologists. And soil specialists. The fish and game people. The recreational effects of cutting have to be addressed, and the winter range of big game.

"And there are the trees to worry about. Blowdowns, bark beetles, fire, insect epidemics. Finally, we have to come up with a management practices plan that covers scenic and recreational uses of the forest. And then, after all that's done, you put the timber up for sale and hope someone buys it."

Like Sinks Canyon, Stillwater State Forest is a big backyard for local people. They fish in it, hunt in it, and compete with bears for huckleberries. Many people buy firewood permits and chop their winter fuel in what Tom Vars counts as a recreational use. "Well, maybe the fathers don't think it's recreation," he said. "But the wife and the kids do. They bring a picnic basket and have fun watching Dad work."

We climbed into a truck for the first of several sorties into his forest, which is far too big for one grand tour. We took a gravel road that soon lost its gravel and then began losing any resemblance to a road. "The trusts," Tom said, shifting to four-wheel drive. "The less we spend on roads, the more money for everything else." We wound through a forest that was all a forest should be—mountainsides bristling with pine and fir and larch, patches of blue shimmering through walls of green, a startled roadside doe transformed into a swift shadow that vanished into the cool dark. We bounced along ruts beside the shore of a lake half a mile long, and saw the boat of one solitary fisherman.

The forest's numerous lakes—Tom says he has never counted them—are the preserve of local people. Fishermen speak guardedly of their favorite spots. Trappers tell no one, including Tom Vars, where they find their marten and their beaver. And if he sees a new beaver lodge, he doesn't tell them. "We're losing beaver," he said. "We're not seeing as many as we used to."

On another trip, we came upon acre after acre of blackened poles that once were trees and rows of charred stumps that bore witness to logging as well as fire. "This is not Stillwater Forest land," he said firmly. "This is a block in private hands. The state sold it in the 1920s, but is no longer allowed to sell any." He paused and looked out over the devastation. "I suppose I should put up a sign saying this is not state forest." He started up the truck. "But signs cost money—and they get shot up."

The day turned drizzly, the kind of day a forester welcomes in fire season. We drove deeper into the forest on a road that was barely a trail, and stopped at a mist-shrouded lake. On it, only a few yards from us, appeared two motionless silhouettes. "Loons," Tom said. "Always the same. One pair to a lake. They're supposed to come back to their own lake every year." He spoke with the quiet authority of someone who knows the ways of a forest by being part of it.

That takes a long time. The casual visitor needs a map, and faith. When Scottie and I first ventured into the forest on our own, we were armed with both. Directional signs helped—when they were there. As Tom says, signs cost money.

Stillwater has undeveloped campgrounds. Each consists of a couple of outhouses and a few scattered campsites, each with a fire pit and a massive picnic table too heavy to be hauled away in a pick-up. Sometimes there is also a garbage can.

Campers come and go as they please. They do not register with anyone. Unlike the campers in a typical national park, they are not gregarious. They seem more interested in getting the boat into the lake than in chatting. There are no programs, no friendly rangers to guide you to the nature trail. There is no nature trail.

For us, much of our Stillwater adventure consisted of stumbling onto the unexpected. Once, as we drove along a narrow ridge, the rugged trail suddenly turned into a newly graded road. We caught up with the grader, perched at the top of a steep hill. We asked the condition of the road below. The man on the grader shook his head. "There are rocks down there that would come up to your hood. You better turn around." As we started back, a black bear climbed up the bank and onto the road. We stopped. The bear stopped. The bear loped away. Not much of an encounter. *But we had seen a bear.*

We had a very different sighting at the edge of a pond. One . . . then two . . . then three muskrats appeared, almost close enough for us to touch them. For a long time we watched them foraging through the reeds. They ducked underwater to snatch a clump of grass, then emerged to crouch and gobble what they found. One of them waddled around with a stalk clamped jauntily in his mouth. When he chomped down on it, we could hear the crackling. Perhaps because of the sense of being alone with wild creatures at our feet, we went back to the pond again and again for the muskrat show.

When the snow comes to Stillwater, so do the snowmobilers, ice fishermen, and cross-country skiers. The forest has four times as many people in winter as in summer. Trappers lay their lines for beaver or marten—or muskrat. Hunters seek moose, elk, deer, and bears, black as well as grizzly. Northwestern Montana is now

131

the only area in the lower 48 states where grizzlies may lawfully be hunted—since 1975, the federal Office of Endangered Species has classified the grizzly as "threatened"—and Vars must monitor the big game in his domain.

Tom Vars believes that his primary mission, sound forestry, helps many animals survive. He talks proudly of the forest's five bald eagle nests: "We don't harvest trees within about an eighth of a mile of their nests or inside the birds' flight patterns. One nest has produced two young every year for three years now." And he showed me how cut-over land had been roughed up to foster natural regeneration.

Vars rarely goes to Glacier National Park, about 40 miles away by road. "I don't have to," he said as he was bidding us good-bye. "We have everything here—except that their peaks are a little higher and we don't have glaciers. But wildlife? We have them beat. You can see more deer, more moose, and more bears on our land than in the park. And a lot fewer people."

Heyburn State Park

But national parks that attract people have become models for many state parks. Some focus on recreation, as a commodity to be produced by wise management. Heyburn State Park in the panhandle of Idaho, for instance, has built a woods-and-waters recreational complex around a true oddity: a river that runs through lakes.

I first saw this phenomenon from a bluff that looked down on what appeared to be a lake almost split in two by a long, sinuous, water-filled island. The "island" turned out to be the St. Joe River, banks and all, coursing along at an elevation of 2,128 feet.

Visitors from near and far are drawn to the isolation of the Idaho Panhandle, a vast wilderness realm within what people in the Northwest call the Inland Empire. At Heyburn, however, visitors get an alternative to wilderness. There is no primitive camping. "The modern camper wants water—even an electrical hookup—and recreation," park manager Fred Bear told me.

And in Heyburn, recreation usually means enjoying the lakes. Families drive to the park with boats in tow. Fishermen try their luck everywhere: in boats, on piers, and on floats anchored well offshore. Motorboats and waterskiers spin around the lakes. The two-stack excursion ship *Coeur d'Alene* carries tourists up the St. Joe and toots at a young fisherman. "Hold up your fish!" the captain calls through a loudspeaker. And a little boy proudly shows off a trophy hardly bigger than his hand. The passengers cheer.

The park's earliest visitors, after 1909, came by steamboat and railroad. Many became summer residents, even full-time residents, by getting state permission to build cottages along the shore or float houses near it. Now 155 cottages stand on leased state land and 28 float homes are moored on leased platforms. When Bill Owens of the park staff took me out in his boat, we passed several float homes. Until they bobbed in our wake, they looked like traditional summer cottages; some had geraniums in window boxes.

Soon after we set out, I could see those surprising mid-lake river-banks. After 1906, I learned, a dam down the valley altered the drainage pattern and raised the level of the water about eight feet. The park's backed-up water became known as four lakes: Round Lake (an elongated blob) northeast of the St. Joe and Chatcolet southeast of it, with extensions called Benewah Lake and Hidden Lake, which got its name when the riverbanks all but sealed it from sight. In recent years, the banks have been eroding. No one knows why, but I noticed that people who did not like speedboats blamed the high wakes that the boats kicked up, and speedboat people blamed the fluctuating water levels caused by a hydroelectric station.

Inevitably, the river is referred to as "the shadowy St. Joe," because cottonwood trees along the banks cast shadows over its waters. It seems strange to pass through shadows in the middle of a lake. Wait . . . *two* lakes, one to port, the other to starboard, each seen through a screen of cottonwoods. The riverbanks have a prairie look—rippling grass, low shrubs, conspicuous trees.

Bill increases power, for suddenly the boat is pushing against a strong river current. A pair of otters slide off a bank, swim around playfully for a moment, and disappear. Ospreys, whistling their plaintive air, soar over the lakes or stare down from riverside trees topped with big, bristling nests. Tree after tree presents the same tableau: sentinel male on high bare branch, female on nest, two or three young peeking over the spiky edge. At least 40 pairs spend their summers in the vicinity, in what may well be North America's largest concentration of this once imperiled bird.

Because of the eroding of the banks, more and more of the ospreys' favorite nesting sites—tall dead trees—are falling into the river. The park has tried pilings as a substitute, and they seem to be working. An osprey eyed us suspiciously from a nest built on a piling so close to a float house that its residents do not need binoculars to watch the nestlings. "She knows me and knows the boat," Bill said. "Otherwise she'd be screaming at us."

Three boys fishing from a float raft proudly held up their string when our boat chugged by. They had caught a dozen or so chubby perch. I asked how they would cook them. "On the barbecue," said Dad, who didn't have time to give me the recipe. He was too busy fishing two windblown jackets out of the water.

So many of the park's quarter-million-a-year visitors prefer the lakes that Scottie and I never met anyone else on the miles of trails that meander through the forests and along the lakeshore. One trail carries hikers back to the 19th century—1859-1862, to be precise, when the U.S. Army hacked a 624-mile military road through the wilderness. This road linked Fort Walla Walla in the Washington Territory with Fort Benton, at the head of low-water navigation on the Missouri River. For three miles we followed the Mullan Trail, named after Lt. John Mullan, who had blazed the way.

When the railroads came, one route followed the Mullan Trail, as did Interstate 90 many years later. Railroads cross the lakes today, but trains pass so infrequently that the tracks are hardly more than relics of the days when railroad kings in the Inland Empire shared power with lumber kings and silver kings. Logging still goes on, but the silver mines have shut down around towns turned ghostly.

About 45 miles from Heyburn, though, we discovered that mining goes on, after a fashion. It's do-it-yourself garnet hunting—at one of the two places on earth where star garnets abound (a district in south-central India is the other). The star garnet, rarer than star rubies or star sapphires, is the Idaho state gem stone.

Armed with borrowed shovels and a screen box for washing gravel, we headed for the Emerald Creek Garnet Area near Clarkia, Idaho. Denise Hudspeth, of the U.S. Forest Service, issued our permits and took us up a trail beside a scarred and muddy slope. Until I saw that mud I had wondered why the leaflet about garnet mining gave the location of the nearest laundromat.

We began chopping away at the slope. "You have to dig down just above bedrock," Denise said, making it sound easy. Dig I did, but all that I shoveled up were some tiny frogs and great globs of mud that oozed back to where it came from. Rarely did I manage to find some likely gravel to sift on the screen box.

Scottie, meanwhile, was having better luck. Hours later, mud-encrusted, squishing, and glittering with mica dust, we weighed our finds on Denise's scale to show that we had not exceeded the five-pound daily limit. The scale registered two ounces.

But two ounces were more than enough for Scottie, who is a potter. As we washed off our hands, faces, and garnets in a nearby stream, she mused like an alchemist over her plans. "The purple kind of garnet," she said, "is mostly iron. I think it'll act like the iron in clay. Iron makes a brown-red stain." She looked at the stones glistening in her clean palm. "I'm going to embed a couple of them in a clay bowl and put a colorless glaze over them when I fire it, and save the memory." Her bowl is now on our mantelpiece, next to a rock.

Rock Hound State Park

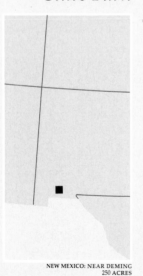

At Rock Hound State Park in southwestern New Mexico, the working conditions were much better. There was no mud. And I easily reached the limit of 15 pounds: the maximum per person, per visit. I reached it several times. That was the problem. You see, I like rocks, and I think they make fine souvenirs of places I have visited. The newer rocks go on shelves or play doorstop in my living room and office; the older ones have been relegated, with full honors, to tasteful arrangements (*not* piles) in the backyard and out front.

I have nothing to show from the national parks I've been in because the National Park Service prohibits the carrying away of federal property, including rocks. In general, state parks have a similar policy, although Crater of Diamonds in Arkansas lets visitors keep any gems they find. Since 1966 Rock Hound State Park has cheerfully encouraged its visitors to dismantle it. (Amateur visitors, that is—commercial collecting is forbidden for "obvious reasons," warns an official brochure.) I naturally looked forward to spending quite some time in this 250-acre park, which consists essentially of a thousand-foot slope strewn with interesting rocks.

Under a stunning blue morning sky, I began my hunt by scrabbling up a scree of sun-bleached rocks. A dark one caught my eye.

I picked it up and put it in my pocket. A few feet higher, I abandoned the treacherous scree for a path. Near a prickly pear, I found a beauty, about half the size of my fist. The rock's pitted surface, under a magnifying glass, was lunar, with tiny crystal craters. The third, gray with streaks of red and brown, was also beautiful. And the fourth. . . .

As I climbed, both the New Mexico sun and the angle of ascent became more punishing. Yet the higher I climbed, the more rocks I picked up. Soon my pockets were full, and I was loading my backpack. About halfway up, I stopped, found some shade by a rock too large to collect, sat down, took a few sips from my canteen, and decided that I had to do something about all the rocks that were weighing me down. Otherwise, I would not be able to climb much higher. So I conducted a Rock Beauty Contest.

I lined up my collection—by now I had 39 rocks—and looked at each one carefully. I put 15 in a tasteful arrangement to my left and the rest in rows to my right. The semifinals were soon over, with 24 contestants remaining. Before beginning the finals, I ate my lunch, resisting the temptation to reconsider any of the runners-up, attractive as they might be.

The finals went more slowly. I reluctantly added 14 to the tasteful arrangement, loaded the 10 finalists in my pack, and climbed on. I know. I could have left the Beautiful Ten behind and picked them up on the way down. But I wanted to be free to wander the slope, which spreads in what geologists call an alluvial fan. Paths exist, but I wanted to try the untrodden. As an experienced rock hound once said of his expeditions, "When we go rock hunting, we walk and walk and don't even start looking until we quit seeing beer cans."

The equivalent of beer cans in this litter-free park were rock piles—and I mean piles—where determined collectors had apparently dug for the large nodules known as thunder eggs and geodes. These treasures, like all the other rocks exposed here, trace their origin to primeval volcanic activity.

In soft, early morning light or in the gloaming, the old volcanic fires gleam in the rocks. The park is in the Little Florida Mountains, whose name (pronounced flor-*ee*-da) suggests the colors—greens and yellows, reds and pinks—locked in the rocks. One theory holds that the mountains got their name from fluorite, a transparent or translucent mineral of many colors. But Frank A. Pena, manager of the park, has his own idea: "I think the mountains were in flower when the Spanish went by here. I think they looked up and, right in the middle of the desert, they saw mountain slopes of flowers. Maybe the Mexican butterscotch poppies—a beautiful carpet of yellow and orange."

Only the scarlet flowers of the ocotillo were bursting forth when I was there. Yucca, barrel cactus, mesquite, and juniper marched along the gullies and filled in between spills of rocks. The ubiquitous cactus made collecting hazardous. When you reach for a rock under a big plant full of needles, sometimes you fail to notice the smaller plants with the unseen prickly fuzz. I could still feel those invisible needles in my fingers days later.

I thought of another peril when, talking with Frank in his rock-filled office, I noticed two large rattlesnake skins nailed to the wall.

"Each one is 56 inches long," Frank said. As he told me about killing the rattlers—"one almost bit me in the face"—I thought of how often I had reached casually into a hollow or blindly past a big rock. "We've only had two people bitten in ten years," he assured me. "They both recovered."

I had found a few more rocks on the climb down and, after one more contest, I had 16 rocks. "We get a lot of beginners," Frank said politely after looking over my assortment. He did not bother to weigh them. (I did, later: just under the limit.)

My best find was a crescent-shaped fragment from what had been a geode, a sort of hardened-mud bubble full of concealed splendor. Within the geode cavity, quartz crystals grow, gradually filling the core—it's the filled kind that's called a thunder egg. My shard contained a sparkling, fractured crystal that mysteriously contracted into darkness, like a tiny treasure cave. Next best was half a sphere, laced inside with tiny red veins that reminded me of the prehistoric drawings found on the walls of caves.

I hastily dumped the others into a bag and mumbled something about not being a collector. "I just like them," I said. Frank nodded, and picked up my favorite. "It *is* pretty," he said, holding it up to the sunlight that streamed through his open door.

Kodachrome Basin State Park

The next rocks I walked among were eerie towers that thrust up from a floor in the high desert country of Utah. As sun and shadow spin out the day, ever-changing shades of red play over the sheer high cliffs that encircle the park. At sunset, the cliff walls quickly become darker than the night. Then the light of a waning moon glazes the spires and the clusters of softly sculptured rock. At morning, the sun is veiled and the world is without shadows. The reds of yesterday are muted. New light and new shadows have brought new colors, new beauty.

This is Kodachrome Basin State Park in Utah, a gem tucked away on a gravel road 22 miles from the immense and thronged Bryce Canyon National Park. "Kodachrome Basin" adequately describes the park, a colorful place, cupped by a small canyon's walls. But to understand and appreciate the park's fragile beauty, I needed a Shakespeare. Luckily, one was there.

Tom Shakespeare, the superintendent, seems to know every square inch of the 2,240 acres. One moment he speaks of the big: the varied colors of distant hills. The next he is focusing on the small: a bobcat's track; a pack rat's jumbled nest of twigs and bark and bits of grass.

He crouches down and points at the reddish, powdery ground. I see nothing in particular until he moves his finger over a funnel-shaped pit half an inch across. "Ant-lion," he says. He pokes at the pit with a blade of grass and something in the pit moves. The two of us crouch over the pit while he tells me about the ant-lion, larva of a flying insect, which had dug the steep-sided pit and buried itself at the bottom, with only its long needle-sharp jaws exposed. There it waits for an ant—or other insect—to fall in. It may even move its body to dislodge a tiny avalanche and bring down its prey. It clamps its jaws on the victim and sucks it dry. Tom points out the body of an ant next to the pit. He sees everything in his park.

And, under his tutelage, I began to see better. Here campers, on an honor system, buy their firewood from a pile of scrap lumber. Silvery, sun-bleached wood lies around as if for the taking. I never want my cook fire to smell and look like something at a construction site. But here there is a good reason to leave even the dead tree trunks and branches untouched. Tom, with his eye on the little, had shown me that these lengths of fallen wood provide tiny worlds of shade and moisture for the unseen creatures trying to make a living in a basin that rarely contains water—for red ants and termites and other insects, for pack rats and lizards.

The basin's major wonders are columns of rock, often called chimneys and known scientifically as sand-pipe intrusions. They occur elsewhere, especially in the Southwest, but this may well be the world's greatest and most spectacular concentration of them. We paused by a tapering chimney, about 30 feet high, that jutted from a clump of Utah junipers. A broad white vein ran up the red sandstone column and bluntly capped it. "By the way," said Tom, "this one has a beehive." Through my binoculars I could see honeycomb sticking out of a large crack, about two-thirds of the way up. Tom, who makes nature trails with such care that they qualify as an art form, had planned one to feature this dramatic tower.

Scientists aren't certain just how these features came into being, or when, but agree that it took a long time for calcite in the groundwater to cement the intrusive sand into a distinctive rock. They also agree that the chimneys came to light recently and rapidly—within, say, the past 10,000 years. "When the soft local sandstone eroded away," Tom said, "the chimneys stayed because they're harder."

At least 67 of these solidified sand pipes dot the park, with more in the vicinity. Their height ranges from 10 to 170 feet, and can change rapidly. "We had one that looked like a seal balancing a ball on its nose," Tom told me. "Then, one winter, the ball fell off." Pieces of another—the 70-ton monster that housed the pack rat's nest—fell away at my unwary touch.

Explorers sponsored by the National Geographic Society named this area "Kodachrome Flat" in 1948. On the same expedition they discovered the spectacular arch that they named for Gilbert H. Grosvenor, then editor of NATIONAL GEOGRAPHIC. Grosvenor Arch is ten miles from the park, which was created in June 1963.

Within the park itself is Shakespeare Arch, which Tom discovered—but did not name. (Shakespeare was the most popular entry in a name-the-arch contest.) In the times of written history, no one noticed the arch until 1977, when Tom, searching for a coyote den, happened upon it. On our walk to the arch, I followed a trail guide that typically reflected Tom's concern with such matters as what plants feed the deer and where wildflowers grow. The guide tells of the discovery of the arch so long unseen and says, "Man has stepped on the moon, yet, how much has he sidestepped on earth?"

The question, I thought, was as much about an arch soaring unseen as about wondrous unseen parks that await discovery at the end of gravel roads.

Sinks Canyon
State Park

Land of contrasts, Sinks Canyon
slices through the Wind River
Range, where evergreen forests
of fir and pine mantle north-facing
slopes while opposite rock walls
support little but a scratchy
covering of sagebrush. Below:
A purple aster pokes from layered
sediments dotted with lichens.
Sinks Canyon takes its name from
the disappearance of the Popo Agie
River into an unmapped cavern.

FOLLOWING PAGES: Trying his luck
at fly fishing, park employee Bill
Ridenour casts for rainbow trout.

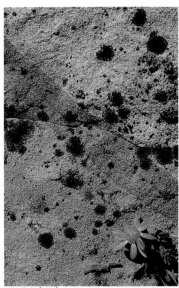

NICK KELSH (BOTH)

139

Stillwater State Forest

A fish's jump—or perhaps the smack of a beaver's tail—ripples the calm waters of Meadow Lake. Lakes not yet counted glimmer in the morning light at Stillwater State Forest, a little-known preserve in northwestern Montana. Meadow Lake tripled in size in the 1970s, thanks to a beaver dam; now moose wade into its shallows to browse. Deer, elk, and bears roam these woods, one of the few areas in the United States that support a population of grizzlies. White plumes of beargrass (below) grow throughout the region; both grizzlies and black bears use the leaves to line their winter dens. While the bears hibernate, the local humans take to the forest for ice fishing, snowmobiling, and cross-country skiing.

Scanning the distance, fire lookout Dave Smith checks the evergreen forests for smoke. "Binoculars suffice for most of my work," says Dave, "but when I see something suspicious, I use the telescope." From his post on Werner Peak, he has a bird's-eye view of 300,000 acres, including Stillwater and part of Flathead National Forest. Squinting into an Osborne Firefinder (bottom right), he demonstrates how to locate a fire by aligning the site within the crosshairs of the Firefinder, a rotating wheel coordinated to compass points and to a map. Stillwater lookouts report about 12 to 16 smokes a year. Lightning ignites most, especially during the dry summer season, when Dave stays at his post weeks at a time. The 14-by-14-foot cabin provides most of the comforts of home (bottom left). "I truly enjoy staying on the lookout," says Dave. "Life's rhythms are set by nature, not a clock. To be honest, I use the telescope most often for watching the moon, sunsets, and wildlife. I work every day if there's a threat of fire or lightning. When it rains, I take some time off." With a day off due, Dave turned over his duties to author Tom Allen and his wife, Scottie, for 24 hours. "Being at the lookout," says Tom, "made me realize the sheer immensity of the forest here."

Heyburn
State Park

Odd but true: The St. Joe River flows through lakes, not land. Wooded riverbanks delineate the river's course through Heyburn State Park in Idaho. This unusual configuration resulted from construction of a dam. As he floats timber to sawmills, a tugboat pilot can easily spot osprey nests in dead cottonwood trees. In one of the largest breeding grounds of the species, Heyburn counts about 80 adults in summer. At right, a

female returns to the nest to watch over her young while her mate searches for fish; she tears his catch into bite-size pieces for the chicks. One parent always stands guard. In September, after the chicks have fledged, the birds migrate to Mexico or farther south for the winter. Come spring, they fly north; the parents will take up residence in their old nest.

Leisure time and the love of nature draw people to the relaxing atmosphere of Heyburn State Park. In a grove of Douglas firs, Tamie Walters plays with her two-year-old son, Raymond. "We enjoy the park all year round," says Tamie, who lives beside Chatcolet Lake. "We love having the lake as a front yard." Approximately 30 people live year round at Heyburn. In the summer the population swells to 1,700 a day. They come to camp, picnic, hike, swim, and play on the lakes at the park—2,000 acres of water. For a July outing, Helen and William Marshall of Nezperce, Idaho, drove their motor home 150 miles to join family and friends at Heyburn. "We belong to an

RV club called the 'Happy Family Campers Club,' " says Helen. "We meet once a month at different recreation areas. Heyburn State Park is on the schedule at least two or three times a year." Below, Helen gives her brother, Wayne Hamilton of Portland, Oregon, a haircut; sister-in-law Myrtle Hamilton watches. Of the friendly poodle that visited their campsite: "She looked like she was waiting to be next for a trim."

PRECEDING PAGES: Yellow bands distinguish state-owned piers from those held by a concession that leases boat sheds to visitors. Anglers and others use all the walkways freely.

Rock Hound State Park / City of Rocks State Park

Monoliths reddened by the dawn form an eerie skyline in City of Rocks State Park. Located in the Chihuahuan Desert of New Mexico, these formations stand as footnotes to the geologic history of the region. More than 30 million years ago, volcanoes blanketed the land with ash and flowing lava that solidified into rock. Over the millennia wind and rain sculpted the stone into a 40-acre cityscape. The Boxing Glove (foreground) towers 50 feet. Nearby, in Rock Hound State Park, the rocks are for the taking. For years Rock Hound prided itself on being the only park in the country that encouraged visitors to take chunks of it home with them. People from across the nation and from Europe,

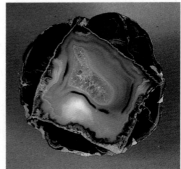

too, come to find semiprecious gemstones. On a busy winter day, as many as 200 people comb a rock-strewn slope hunting for jasper, opal, agates, geodes, and other collector's items. A cut and polished amethyst geode on display in the visitor's center (above) is as big as a basketball.

153

Kodachrome Basin State Park

Rugged beauty, clear horizons: The splendor of Kodachrome Basin bespeaks the wonders of southern Utah. Tucked among such popular recreation areas as Zion, Bryce, and Grand Canyon National Parks, Kodachrome Basin remains a secluded, unspoiled parkland. On a spring afternoon, riders on horseback have the park's only road to themselves as they amble through the Grand Parade of Spires, where pinyon jays chatter in juniper trees and eagles soar above free-standing sandstone formations called chimneys. Rich natural colors and shifting patterns of light prompted explorers to name the area during a 1948 expedition sponsored by the National Geographic Society. Today, as then, the state parks and preserves of the Rocky Mountain region continue to challenge the camera and capture the imagination.

SNOW AND SUN IN

THE FAR WEST

By Seymour L. Fishbein
Photographs by David Alan Harvey

157

Chugach State Park

Anchorage, the metropolis of Alaska, sprawls over a million acres. Half of them accommodate the urban web. Almost all the rest is Chugach State Park. City folk head for it right from the office, to hike or ski. They enjoy its wildlife, on the hoof or on the table. Occasionally its wildlife enjoys Anchorage, nibbling in suburban gardens, ambling into town. So in a sense the 780-square-mile state park is a city park as well. But it's also Alaska.

On the fifth day of a two-and-a-half-day winter outing in the park, Chris Johns poked deep down in his pack for something to eat. To his delight his numb fingers closed around a granola bar. "For a second," Chris recalled, "I thought, 'Gad, I'm the weakest of the bunch, maybe I just ought to eat it.' Then, 'No! What's wrong with you. We've got to split it.' "

The bunch included guide Gary Bocarde, who had scaled Mount McKinley more than a dozen times, and Mike Frank, an assistant attorney general for the state, who spends many a winter weekend skiing and camping. They were scarcely 30 miles from high-rise Anchorage, yet held fast in the Chugach. Clouds shrouded the site of their ski-plane rendezvous. The famed Iditarod Trail lay a few miles away, but icefalls and avalanche-primed slopes blocked the approaches. Food was almost gone. Still, the granola would go into reserve. No telling when or how they would come out.

Chris Johns is no weakling. A veteran ice climber in the Cascades, he had arranged a tour of Eagle Glacier to photograph the park backcountry in its winter prime. Around the Chugach fringes, however, no mountaineer's strength is needed to ski and camp, as I did one February weekend. Here in the biting air and slowly lengthening days I began a tour of western parks, from giant Chugach to a tiny sliver of Alaskan Native culture, from a turbulent sliver of California coast to a mountainous desert aflame with spring. In summer I kayaked alongside Hawaiian sea cliffs and climbed, on horseback, an alpine corner of northeastern Oregon.

The bold Chugach rim provides a daily pick-me-up to urban Anchorage. At dawn the mountains appear as a shadowy massif in the east, where the street lights end abruptly. As city lights fade, peaks and ridges define themselves; veins of snow crease dark slopes. Soon, sunbeams flare behind the mountains; in backlight the range flattens to a cutout silhouette, an image overexposed.

Beyond that hypnotic facade stretches an icy park wilderness, the western end of the 300-mile-long Chugach Mountains, which contain a fourth of Alaska's glacier-covered terrain.

Eagle Glacier was a cloudless joy on the Monday morning Chris,

Turbulent Turnagain Arm, funneling cold winds and water, tests the most skilled windsurfers. At times, bore tides rush in as walls of water.
PRECEDING PAGES: Off to a sunny start, an Eagle Glacier outing turned into a week-long ordeal as a winter storm trapped the skiers in the Chugach wilds.

Gary, and Mike landed there. "I couldn't shoot fast enough. It was so gorgeous, so remote. The surface was terrific. I did the most telemark turns I've ever done, skiing the best I've ever skied. Gary cooked a terrific meal. We ate like kings."

But with the halibut course came the snow. Steady wind and snow, through the night. Tuesday was whiteout day, leaving them comfortably tent-bound, the temperature well below freezing, but tolerable. Wednesday was getaway day, but no planes would find Eagle Glacier then. The campers scouted a route to the trail that might let them ski out, southward toward Crow Pass and the community of Girdwood.

As they tracked beyond a shallow slope, a freak avalanche broke loose and caught them, burying Gary and Chris to their armpits, Mike to the top of his head. They could see more snow hanging up-hill. If that came down, they were finished. Mike was set in concrete; without help, he would simply freeze. He was well iced down by the time the other two freed themselves and got to him.

That route was out. They started rationing food. Thursday was the worst yet, a razor wind, the whiteout solid. Friday looked promising. They packed up, and roped up, and set out for a hut sited on the glacier for just such emergencies. For a while they wandered in soup so thick the end men on the 165-foot rope could not see each other. They left the hut Saturday morning to seek a way down Eagle Glacier to the Eagle River Visitor Center.

The center, however, lay some 16 miles distant and 4,000 feet below them, beyond ice blocks the size of apartment houses. They probed for crevasses in a total whiteout. A certain grimness set in as they made camp. Chris was cramped and frostbitten and could not stop shivering, even in his sleeping bag, even after filling up on hot water. That was dinner. The question of survival came up.

And then came Sunday, to answer all questions. The ceiling lifted. Just as they started out, they heard the ski-plane. Not until then did they divide and devour the granola bar.

For my weekend of ski camping, the hard part was getting into the Chugach, not getting out. I set out one February morning for the South Fork of Eagle River with Mike Frank, Superintendent Bill Garry, and environmental activist Cliff Eames. A few steps beyond road's end I began to feel out of place. Downhill is my game, nice downhill intermediate skiing, always yielding the honor of defying gravity to chair lifts. Now here we were, laden with packs, switch-backing uphill—or trying to. Bill had detoured to avoid trespassing on private land. As the others climbed and I tunneled on all sixes—skis, knees, and hands—two shots rang out. And a voice called from a house downhill: "I can get serious if you want."

"We'll have to go back," said Bill, eyes glowering between his red beard and brows. He thought he had cleared private land. A homesteader disagreed, with some noisy rhetoric. We retreated.

The shoot-out on the South Fork touches on the jagged problem of park access. On occasion, at established entry points off O'Malley Road, visitors jam trailheads and nearby streets. At other places, splendid valleys have little or no public access. And landowners are wary of trespassers and vandals.

But homesteaders blasting away? What century is this? I learned that before 1969 you could claim a 160-acre patch of tilted wilderness from the federal government for a small filing fee. If you built a simple dwelling, cultivated an eighth of the tract, planted something or other, and toughed it out for three years, the land was yours. By the mid-1980s you were no longer sitting on giveaway wilderness. You were beside a half-million-acre state park, a short commute from spreading Anchorage. And the view, observed a homesteader friend as we watched sunbeams bouncing off the picture window of his privy, was unbeatable. A 160-acre tract, subdivided, could turn a homesteader into a millionaire.

Stymied at the South Fork, our party worked around to Ship Creek, another of the park's 15 major valleys. We clambered down a hillside, then skied over willow thickets and crusty snow for a mile to camp on a sunny ledge just below tree line, at around 2,000 feet.

Cliff and Mike spread mats on the snow and, like votaries at a shrine, knelt before their little stoves, priming, cursing, coaxing blue flame at last. With enough melted snow, we could proceed to cream of broccoli soup and a subtle, fragrant pesto. With the temperature near zero, leisurely dining is out; you start on the noodles right off the stove; before you finish they are freezing to the bowl.

What Mike and Cliff taught me to savor at leisure was the wilderness. They are tireless advocates. When a helicopter coursed the valley, a barrage of verbal flak went up, some aimed at the chopper, some at Bill Garry for tolerating it. Wildlife had a narcotic effect; glimpses of moose, raven music, ptarmigan sign, the repartee of unseen songbirds, all seemed to draw quiet satisfaction.

Dusk settled over Ship Creek, but darkness never came. Before the sun vanished a full moon rose to spread a brassy sheen across the piebald slopes. Then Orion spread-eagled the sky, much as the poet Robinson Jeffers had seen him: "strung in the throat of the valley like a lamp-lighted bridge."

I took a water bottle into my sleeping bag. Mike asked me to, so that in the morning he could begin with water instead of snow. This sped the moment when he could present his filtered, fresh-ground Kenya roast—with bagels fried in butter. Like cold-blooded animals, we basked until the sun warmed us. Then we skied out.

Chugach State Park is more than a winter's tale. In mid-April, while much of the park lies under deep snow, wild celery and currants are green and blooming on the south-facing slopes above Turnagain Arm, the park's southern water boundary. It's like traveling a thousand miles south, says Peter Martin, who worked as a forester for the state parks until he retired. Soon Anchorage comes out to Turnagain Arm en masse for the first spring run of fish, the oily little eulachon, or hooligan. Summer brings nesting songbirds and wildflowers, and berries free for the picking. Fall colors come and go quickly. "The supreme moment," says Pete Martin, "occurs on that rare day or two when the autumn birches stand in full glory—gold against the pure white of the Chugach peaks."

Few state parks can match the spaciousness of Chugach. Yet it is only a third the size of 1.5-million-acre Wood-Tikchik, largest state park in Alaska and second to Adirondack in the nation. This giant preserve is part of the great Bristol Bay salmonry of southwestern Alaska, with luxurious fishing lodges for the executive-jet set.

Totem Bight State Historical Park

ALASKA: NEAR KETCHIKAN
11 ACRES

In the opposite direction, a rich fishing culture of a very different kind is reflected along a bend, or bight, of the Tongass Narrows near Ketchikan. Eleven acres small, Totem Bight State Historical Park remembers an affluent society that fished and hunted, danced in elegant regalia, held lavish feasts that went on for days, and patronized the arts. The society is that of the Tlingits and Haidas, Northwest Coast tribes, and a semblance of their art survives today in the totem poles and plank house on a grassy sward between water's edge and the evergreen rain forest.

The dwelling represents a traditional clan house for a chief and several families; its facade bears a carving of Raven—most powerful of all creatures of legend. Creator of man, prankster, hero of many a tale, Raven had moves that children dream of: He could live inside a whale, rocket to the heavens, turn himself into whatever he chose—man, woman, hemlock needle.

On house corners sit two carved men with conical hats, useful for shedding rain in an area that receives 160 inches a year. The men wear painted designs on their faces. Time for a potlatch, they're saying, let the feasting begin.

Even without a potlatch there were good times here. The site is said to have attracted generations of Tlingits in summer. Here they could rake herring and gather shellfish at the shore, net salmon from a creek, hunt mammals in the woods and in the waters offshore.

Today the summer visitors are mostly cruise passengers. They come by the busload from Ketchikan for a closer look at this legacy of art and legend.

Until half a century ago it was a disappearing legacy, as Indians abandoned remote villages. Unwilling to see the monuments lost, Native communities and U.S. Forest Service employees joined forces to save them. Skilled elders trained a new generation of carvers. Poles were restored or copied and set up in parks. Ketchikan, with Totem Bight and another totem park at nearby Saxman, and the Totem Heritage Center within the city, has become a lively shrine of Northwest Coast art and remembrance.

Nathan Jackson makes it even more so. Born Yelch Yedi—Raven Child—in the Chilkoot-Tlingit tribe, he spent part of his youth in traditional pursuits, hunting seals, fishing at summer camps. "I was my grandfather's strong right arm," he recalls. But the old man was hard to please. "You'll never amount to anything," he told the frustrated teenager. So much for the wisdom of the elders. Today Nathan is a master carver. His poles and panels are all over Alaska, in Seattle and Salt Lake City, in Japan and England. And he is not without honor in Ketchikan. Warm smiles and handshakes greet the graying, compactly built artist wherever he goes in this waterfront town.

At his carver's shed and in the dripping woodland at Totem Bight I learned from Nathan something of his art: how a log of western red cedar—its softness and even grain make it the choice over spruce and hemlock—is transformed into an evocation of myth, legend, and folk memory.

Totem Bight illustrates this rich lore. There were welcome poles to greet canoes at water's edge, mortuary poles, and potlatch poles. Ridicule poles were put up to harass an adversary. Heraldic poles displayed clan crests and recounted ancestral adventures. With a little coaching it is not hard to pick out the stylized animals in the tales. Raven has a straight beak, Eagle a curved one. Gnawing teeth identify Beaver, and so on. Only initiates, however, can interpret the full story on a pole.

At Totem Bight a simple pole tells the tragic tale of the human, Kats, and his Bear wife. The shaft displays only paw prints; on top of it crouches the grizzly wife. She had warned Kats not to look on the human wife he had deserted. When he did, his cub children tore him to pieces. At this the Bear wife departed, singing a dirge as she slowly climbed a mountain.

And there are her tracks, climbing. And there she sits, high on the pole, looking down.

A few years ago, when the grizzly figure decayed, Israel Shotridge was chosen to carve a replacement. He had grown to manhood with no sense of his Tlingit heritage. "All I could see," he told me, "was dollar signs." But when he apprenticed himself to Nathan Jackson, "a whole world opened up." Israel took courses in Tlingit at the community college, started dancing, acquired regalia. When he completed his carving, Israel enlisted a bird with Raven powers. From a nearby tree he signaled the helicopter that set the figure in place. He climbed down, donned regalia—leggings, bear mask, and headdress—and grasped an adz in one hand and a knife in the other. Then, while his mother beat the drum and friends looked on, Israel danced the carver's dance of his Tlingit forefathers.

Anza-Borrego Desert State Park

From soggy, wintry southeastern Alaska I flew to a desert corner of California. There were stops in between, but they could wait. In March, Anza-Borrego is fresh and balmy, sprinkled with color. Here 600,000 acres surround the serene valley town of Borrego Springs, 87 miles' drive east of San Diego. The granite Peninsular Ranges rise abruptly, wringing moisture from Pacific winds before they sweep eastward over the desert. In summer the mountains deflect sultry southerly winds, loosing cloudbursts and flash floods in the canyons and dry washes.

Along uncrowded roads roll motor homes, long and luxurious. More than a dozen campgrounds dot the park. At the more popular ones, weekend campsite spaces in flower season are scarcer than raindrops in June, when temperatures climb into triple digits and rainfall averages zero. Backpackers can bed down almost anywhere in the park, though the need to lug water may limit their range.

Rainy Alaska and desert California, so distant and disparate, are linked by historic stirrings that echo in the name of Anza-Borrego. In the late 1760s Spain heard of a threat to her Pacific domain: The Russians were coming, coming down the coast from Alaska in search of sea otters and their silky pelts. Determined to reinforce her outposts in Alta (Upper) California, Spain sought a land route from northern Mexico to the Pacific shore. In March 1774 *Capitán* Juan Bautista de Anza and a scouting party camped by a marshy sink in southeastern California. Ahead, to the west, lay the expanse that enshrines his name—the wide, sandy washes; the gray buttes and gnarled

CALIFORNIA: NEAR SAN DIEGO
600,000 ACRES

badlands; the broad, rising Borrego Valley; San Ysidro Mountain on the west, the Santa Rosas on the north, and the gap between them, Anza's gateway to the coast.

Northwest up Coyote Canyon he marched, crossing the gap near 6,193-foot Combs Peak, highest point in the park. Completing his pioneering trek, Anza returned a year later with settlers, their wives and about 125 children, bound for the presidio of Monterey. High up Coyote Canyon, the First Child Monument marks the spot where, on Christmas Eve in 1775, Salvador Ygnacio Linares was born, a non-Indian native of California. Anza, writes a 20th-century historian, was the first European trailblazer "to lead a colony overland to the North Pacific shores."

Coyote Canyon remains a rough, wild passage, though you can drive partway up today. The vehicle will buck like an unbroken horse as it lurches up Coyote Creek, dodging boulders, whacking willow tangles, flopping into ruts. An ugly roadbed, to be sure—but what a roadside. While park naturalist Mark Jorgensen jockeyed his jeep up-creek one day, I sat tight and enjoyed the flower show: sand verbena, monkey flowers, desert dandelion, chicory. Domes of yellow flowers capped the brittlebush, whose resin the Spanish padres used for incense. Green wands tipped with orange-red blooms rose everywhere. This is the ocotillo—little torch, clothed with leaf and sparked into flame by late-winter rains.

In summer no visitor may enter the canyon. The park's name hints at the reason. *Borrego* means "lamb" in Spanish. Four hundred desert bighorns—lambs, rams, and ewes—roam ridges and canyons here. In the summer heat they descend to seek water. They tank up every few days, Mark told me, taking on as much as five gallons. "They go in very gaunt. You can see all their ribs. They look near dead. When they come away, they look all sleek and bloated."

No *borreguero* tends his flock more devotedly than Mark. This shepherd studies his bighorns, lobbies for them, would even kill for them. His targets are the cows stranded in the canyons when the park acquired new land and banned cattle grazing on it in 1971. They trample habitat, he insists, and they may be transmitting diseases to the wild sheep. They seem to be reproducing themselves. Top-notch cowboys can't lure or herd them out. For Mark, the most practical solution would be to shoot the cattle and leave them for the coyotes.

Not everyone agrees. Not cattlemen. Not California law, which makes it a felony to kill livestock. Not ol' Vern Whitaker, a grizzled Oklahoma cowboy who donates his time and skill to run the corral near Coyote Canyon. "Cows belong here," he insists. "They mow the grass. Sheep smell up the park."

During a truce in the range wars, an expensive solution evolved —a plan to knock out the cattle with dart guns and lift them out by helicopter. A drain on the taxpayers, fumes Mark, but what can you do? "We've exhausted every other means."

In general, however, the taxpayers have gotten a much better park than they paid for. The striking visitor center near Borrego Palm Canyon, built underground to suggest the burrowing lifeways of desert creatures, cost more than a million dollars. Taxpayers paid half; park enthusiasts, acting through the Anza-Borrego Desert Natural History Association, put up the other half. In their yards volunteers nursed cactuses and other plants, then set them out in a spacious garden around the center.

Many of these volunteers are resident retirees, or snowbirds with winter homes here, delighting in slow-paced, uncrowded Borrego Springs and its breathtaking surroundings. "These are people, by and large, who create their own excitements," says Harry Daniel, a retired Virginia businessman and an association leader. He also belongs to George's Geriatric Slaveys, or Fossils Hunting Fossils, whose members scour the badlands for relics of mammoths, horses, camels, sabertooths, and other creatures that roamed the green savannas and woodlands here in Ice Age days.

George—George J. Miller, curator of paleontology at the Imperial Valley College Museum—leads the fossil hunts. These are serious without being dreary. One day, as George surveyed sediments in the Borrego Badlands, his slaveys chipped away with their hammers. Now and then they paused to inhale the fragrance of desert lavender, to admire the chartreuse haze of the paloverde trees coming into bloom, to convene at a dark little hole where a sidewinder snoozed. And to wonder what surprises Julie Parks might have in store. The "Perle Mesta of the desert" needs little excuse to cap a fossil hunt with a party. This day, as the sun neared the zenith, she broke out fresh strawberries and cold champagne and orange juice. "What's the occasion?" I asked. "It's hot out," she replied.

People often spoke of the desert silence, the intense, magical silence. A good place to experience it, suggested Mark Jorgensen, was Font's Point. So we rode out in his jeep, late one afternoon, to the scarp above the shadowed badlands. Spectacular vistas look eastward toward the Salton Sea, north and west to the Peninsular Ranges. Instead of silence at twilight, we found a desert happy hour in progress. Some winter migrants had set up a portable picnic table. As the men recycled war stories and the women talked of summer plans, someone suddenly pointed to the sun teetering on a ridge of San Ysidro. Up went the libations: "Bye bye, sun." With that the celebrants folded the table and sauntered off into the dusk. And left the mesa and the badlands to the coyotes and kit foxes, to the rattlers and the iguanas. A few birds were still at evensong. In the pauses between the songs I heard the silence of the desert.

Unknown to Captain Anza, there was an easier route across the mountains. Kit Carson scouted it for the army in 1846, during the Mexican War. It became the first wagon route across southern California and, in time, the Southern Emigrant Trail. Mementos of struggling wagoneers and stagecoach days dot the park, some well off the beaten track. One day I nosed a van down Canyon Sin Nombre— Canyon Without a Name—and ground over sandy, rocky washes in four-wheel drive to the site of the old Carrizo Stage Station. In 1937 the master photographer Edward Weston paused here. He found a few adobe bricks, a eucalyptus tree, a cottonwood—and a dead man. "Hunger and privation had wasted his body and the merciless sun had dried him up," Weston wrote. "But he was quite beautiful in death." Weston photographed him, an unforgettable image. There is no sign of him at the site today, nor much of anything else. But the eucalyptus is still there, a handsome old patriarch with a few limbs in good leaf, standing tall on the desert horizon.

Point Lobos State Reserve

CALIFORNIA: NEAR CARMEL
1,200 ACRES (450 ACRES ON LAND,
750 ACRES UNDERWATER)

From Anza-Borrego I traveled north to another California parkland, a fragment of rock and sea met in roaring crescendo, where Weston spent some of the most fruitful days of his life.

It lies at the edge of the Monterey Peninsula. Here the explorer Sebastián Vizcaíno, an early master of California hype, reported the discovery of a *puerto famoso*—a fine port "sheltered from all winds." In fact Monterey Bay is an open roadstead. Nonetheless the site became the capital of Alta California, Anza's goal.

Just to the south the Spaniards beheld a gathering of sea mammals and heard their barking and named a headland Punta de los Lobos Marinos. We call the animals sea lions, not sea wolves. But the Spanish name and the sights and sounds remain, among natural splendors crammed into two square miles.

One raucous day, as March blew in like a lion, I sat in a sheltered rock hollow and looked out beyond the point, beyond the chalk-white moil of Devil's Cauldron. There they were, lolling on Sea Lion Rocks, their hoarse cacophony rolling in over the thunder of the breakers. I scanned the open sea; after a few minutes I saw a spout rise—a gray whale migrating northward. And a minute later, on a park road, I strolled behind a hummingbird foraging for nectar in seaside painted cup. So goes Point Lobos State Reserve, from great whales to tiny hummingbirds.

The red flower and green bird were not the only bright spots along the roads and trails: footsteps-of-spring, of course, in this season; star zygadene, with its white star blossoms; fragrant blue tufts of *Ceanothus thyrsiflorus*, wild lilac. And the unmistakable *copa de oro*—cup of gold—the California poppy.

In quiet coves, where the morning sun turned the sea to beaten silver, fat harbor seals basked on the rocks, cormorants hung their wings to dry, gulls tacked into the wind—the "wave-gleaners" Robinson Jeffers saw from his stone house across Carmel Bay.

Edward Weston moved into the nearby art-colony town of Carmel in December 1928. On May 14, 1930, he wrote in his daybook: "Point Lobos yesterday. . . . I never tire of that wonder spot. . . . I decided to work with cypress for the first time in months: the sun on their weather-polished trunks reveals every tiny line, etched black on a surface glistening as ivory."

As he wrote, so he photographed them, studies of form and texture and light, studies of survival on wind-beaten, spume-wracked, salt-burned granite cliffs. And so the Monterey cypresses stand, clinging to cliff's edge, condescending to the sea winds, leaning landward, seemingly dead. Some are—tumbled to earth, or still standing with whirligig limbs spiraling up into the sky. But often a twisted bole, bending low, finds a sheltered space uphill, where a few green limbs sport the dignified bonsai look of living cypresses.

Monterey cypress grows easily as an ornamental, even as a timber crop. But in the wild the species exists only at Point Lobos and at Cypress Point on the Monterey Peninsula—no other conifer in the world has so small a natural range.

Point Lobos is never crowded. "On any given day," says supervising ranger Glenn McGowan, "we let 450 people in and close the gate." When someone leaves, another may enter. And no one stays overnight. At Whalers Cove and Bluefish Cove scuba divers—45 maximum at any one time—may explore an array of starfish and other forms of tide-pool life.

Creative photographers seek out the rocks and trees that inspired Weston. Interest ran especially high in 1986, his centennial year; a stretch of shore at Lobos was formally dedicated as Weston Beach. I asked Cole Weston, youngest of Edward's four sons, himself a photographer, to walk it with me.

Part of this shore consists of multihued pebbles, set in a matrix or heaped loosely along the beach. There are also uptilted layers of shale and sandstone, rippled tones of gray and brown. "Incredible forms," remarked Cole. What did his father do with those forms that others haven't done? "He made us perceive them the way he perceived them. He had wonderful eyes. Through his artistry, through his vision, he could make people see rocks like they'd never seen rocks before." Or cypresses and seashells and desert dunes.

On New Year's Day, 1958, Weston died of Parkinson's disease. He was cremated, and the four sons came down to this beach with his ashes. By themselves. "I just took the ashes," said Cole as we watched the sea cream over the pebbles and the layered rock, "and strewed them out over the water. Then we went back to the studio and toasted him. And that was it."

A nd that was it for spring. On to summer. I had not seen Hawaii since the 1940s, and then only for a day or so, wallowing in self-pity as I left. In the Navy, Hawaii was always good duty. It still is. At least I found it so when I joined the minifleet of Micco Godínez and his friend Vicki Newberry to see the world of Kauai, next-to-westernmost of the main islands. We paddled two inflatable kayaks, Micco with a supply canoe in tow. There were grander flotillas at sea, thick-skinned Zodiacs heaped to their puffy gunwales with tourists. There were sight-seeing helicopters overhead, roaring into magnificent canyons. Such awesome power. Such noise. I was never tempted to desert.

A coastal road loops Kauai, from Haena State Park in the north to the hot beaches of Polihale State Park in the west. Between the two there is no road, only *na pali*—the steep cliffs. Along the 14-mile strip of Na Pali Coast State Park marine erosion has chewed away the weaker lavas of the ancient shield volcano that formed Kauai. Sheer cliffs rise as high as 4,000 feet. Streams have cut 22 major valleys in the pali; weathering has pleated the rock face, as if miles of drapery had been drawn across the cliffs.

From Haena a rough 11-mile trail winds up and down along the coast to the valley of Kalalau. Before embarking with Micco I spent a delightful rainy morning on the trail with Superintendent George Niitani. I think he enjoyed it too, taking great glee from my haole—non-Hawaiian—pronunciation of native words. "You people talk so funny." He laughed. I laughed. *Me* talk funny? Wild.

Along the trail I had seen broad leaves wrapped around stones. "Those are leaves of the ti plant," said George, "put down by hikers as an offering to the gods, to bring good luck." As we walked, George

Na Pali Coast State Park

HAWAII: ON KAUAI
4,895 ACRES

167

recounted the lore of the lush plant life: the hala, with its stiltlike roots; the kukui, the state tree; the ohia-lehua, with its sacred red flower. "You may not pick a flower of the ohia-lehua," he warned, "unless you first offer it to the goddess of fire, Madam Pele. If you don't do that, it will rain on you forever." The rain beat down. There was not a single flower on the tree. Hmmmm. . . .

Walking alone, I slogged up a muddy, bouldery valley trail to see Hanakapiai Falls foaming down its lava wall for 800 feet. Weary and bruised, I stripped and sat in the cool, windy plunge pool, and shivered, and stared.

From the cliffs the kayaks look tiny and tippy. In fact they're stable and forgiving, and a foot-controlled rudder makes it possible to steer without interrupting the rhythm of paddling. For most paddlers, however, the seas along this coast are too rough in all but the summer months.

With a steady push from the northeast trade winds, we paddled nine miles to Milolii and set up camp on the beach. Then, with boats light, we worked back up coast for day hikes, starting early, when the wind against us was mildest. In the afternoon we coasted home, bobbing at times on a whitecapped sea, flying before winds of 20 knots or more. The kayaks loved it all.

At Nualolo Kai we snorkeled among the reef fishes, a dazzle of color and grace. We played in wave-chiseled sea caves, and in lava tubes, where the soft center of ropy pahoehoe lava had been squeezed out. From rock ledges white-capped noddies eyed us nervously. Flying fishes, silvery blue, skimmed the waves. High above the hanging valleys, white-tailed tropicbirds sailed on saber wings.

At broad Kalalau Valley, beach, cave, and woodland attract campers. In a green bower a fine waterfall serves as community shower. It is much in demand. When we passed by one day, we found a merry assemblage of young bodies—some washing, some dressing, some undressing. Kalalau is known for its laissez-faire dress code. "Is it a problem?" I asked George Niitani one day. "Not at all," he shook his head. "We used to go around like that all the time, until the missionaries came out here."

One day at Milolii a few local fishermen showed up with rods and spear guns. In Hawaii one queries fishermen cautiously. For it is known that fish can hear, and the usual chitchat will scare them off. So I went a bit roundabout with young Matt Munar. "How's it going?" I asked, glancing toward the tackle. Matt smiled. He had already been out on the reef. Opening his spacious cooler, he pointed to a mullet, a goatfish, and a parrot fish. "This one we call Sleeping Jesus," he said. "When he sleeps, he has a big, white—" Matt swung his arms to describe a halo. Of course. The parrot fish spreads a protective bubble of mucus while it sleeps.

Our time was up. We paddled four downwind miles to the park boundary at Polihale. There we waited for our ride among Hawaiians encamped on the beach. We talked of the valleys we'd climbed, and of the goats they had hunted in those valleys. We sampled their goat-meat stew, and washed it down with their beer. A stroller joined us, glanced at the kayaks, then at Micco, Vicki, and me. "You paddle all the way from Haena?" Yup. Big smile: "Heyyy! You're royal Hawaiians. Haoles use the motor." Made my day.

The fish must be deaf in northeastern Oregon. At Wallowa Lake, tucked below the lordly mountains that feed it, everybody talks about the fish: where they're biting, what they're biting, why they're not biting. The very name of lake and range recalls an old fishing technique. When spawning salmon choked the streams, Nez Perce Indians anchored their nets on each bank with a tripod of poles, which they called a *wallowa*.

At Wallowa Lake today the fishing is with bait and hook—"yankin'," the local people say—and it is not so easy as it used to be. But on those days that all fishermen know, when the line never snaps taut, there is much to see and reflect upon here.

Wallowa Lake State Park, with its marina and more than 200 campsites set amid cottonwoods, spruces, and pines, rims the south end of the lake. Southward rises the great scarp of the Wallowa Mountains. They have a raw young look, rough-hewn and cuspy. At the base of the escarpment, an Ice Age glacier heaped morainal mounds of rock and sediment. When the ice finally disappeared, it left a textbook example of a glacial lake, a mile wide and four miles long. Lateral moraines along the east and west shores rise a thousand feet above the water. A lower terminal moraine hems the northern shore, and glacial outwash fans across the valley.

Damming the northern outlet for irrigation cut off spawning runs from the sea. The lake today offers anglers the landlocked salmon called kokanee, rainbow trout, and the mackinaw, or lake trout, which runs big and runs deep. Visitors also course the lake in paddle-boats, water ski, and plunge into the cool waters. Some wend their way into the mountains, whose names resound with history.

In 1877, when the army came to clear the Nez Perce from their cherished Wallowa country, young Chief Joseph and his band began their epic retreat, battling for a thousand miles before surrendering to Gen. O. O. Howard. From the lake the horizon evokes both leaders. Chief Joseph Mountain rises to the southwest, Mount Howard to the southeast.

I walked the trails on Chief Joseph, and on horseback climbed a valley beside Howard, entering the Eagle Cap Wilderness of Wallowa-Whitman National Forest. I rode up into woodlands of larch and fir and pine, across fell-fields of jumbled boulders. I heard the music of snowmelt cascading down the valleys, choirs of winter wrens, Swainson's thrushes, and ruby-crowned kinglets. Often, I looked down at the dark blue body of Wallowa Lake.

This alpine enchantment was journey's end in the western parks. The journey had been far-ranging and full of contrasts, yet its meaning is simple, compressed in a few lines by Robinson Jeffers:

> *Look—and without imagination, desire nor dream—directly*
> *At the mountains and sea. Are they not beautiful? . . .*
> > *Look at the Lobos Rocks off the shore,*
> *With foam flying at their flanks, and the long sea-lions*
> *Couching on them. Look at the gulls on the cliff-wind,*
> *And the soaring hawk under the cloud-stream—*
> *But in the sagebrush desert, all one sun-stricken*
> *Color of dust, or in the reeking tropical rain-forest,*
> *Or in the intolerant north and high thrones of ice—is the earth*
> > *not beautiful?*

Wallowa Lake State Park

OREGON: NEAR JOSEPH
160 ACRES

Chugach
State Park

Spring lambing over, Dall's sheep ewes and their young nibble and nuzzle on park cliffs, within view of Turnagain Arm and the busy highway that links Seward and Anchorage. King of the hill, the ram bestrides his pedestal like a living trophy. The size of his horns determines his dominance standing among his peers; this fine set would probably rank him in the top tenth of the hierarchy. The curl, coming almost full circle, makes him a legal target elsewhere in the park, but not in this off-limits corner.

FOLLOWING PAGES: *Alaska Air Mushers rise at sunset over Anchorage. Beyond, Rabbit Creek divides the Chugach peaks. At left, unnamed summits flank Ptarmigan, a climber's favorite.*

CHRIS JOHNS (ALL)

CHRIS JOHNS

Totem Bight
State Historical Park

Uncraven raven alights on Raven, legendary creator, most powerful of creatures, and wily antagonist. Bird and superbird top the clan house entrance pole (below) at the totem park near Ketchikan, Alaska, where the carver's art preserves tales of the Tlingit and Haida Indians. Beneath Raven's feet lies the box with daylight, which he delivered to a dark world. In front of the house rises a welcome pole; Grizzly Bear, low man on this totem pole, displays fierce claws— useless against the pranks of Raven. The Thunderer (opposite) made lightning flash with a blink of his eyes; when he stirred his wings, the heavens quaked.

TOM BEAN (ALL)

Anza-Borrego Desert State Park

DAVID MUENCH (ABOVE)

With winter rains, the ocotillo flames: Gaunt, spiny stalks leaf out and flaunt their fiery tips. Indians burned ocotillo for torchlight; settlers planted it for cattle fencing. Remnants of an old ocotillo corral still stand in Anza-Borrego's Coyote Canyon. Though winter brings scarcely an inch of rain per month, that amount produces a brilliant flower show. Gray, brittle stems of brittlebush quicken into bloom (lower right), gilding entire hillsides in the park. Whatever the season, California fan palms (right) signal the presence of water nearby, even if unseen; for, as the saying goes, the desert palm grows with its "feet in water and its head in the sun." The drooping dead fronds provide cooling insulation and also a nickname—petticoat palm.

FOLLOWING PAGES: Font's Point crowns badlands wizened by desert winds and summer cloudbursts. Ancient lake and Colorado River sediments formed these hills; faulting rippled the land with mountain barriers and low-lying basins, such as Borrego Valley (in the middle distance), where Juan Bautista de Anza and his pioneer settlers marched in 1775. The viewpoint, one of the most popular in the park, honors Father Pedro Font, Anza's diarist and sorely tried chaplain of an expedition eager to relieve the desert rigors with sinful fandangos.

How's ol' Vern? Still up at the horse camp? Rangers of Anza-Borrego field such questions again and again, and are happy to answer: Just fine. Still up there, his face making no secret of his 75 years. Still riding that six-gaited Peruvian paso of his, part of the Coyote Canyon landscape along with the beavertail cactus and the buckhorn cholla and the creosote bush. Still full of the cowboy yarns from Oklahoma, where he started riding at the age of five. Still putting in 200 hours a month, all

volunteer time, seeing to the corral he built and the visitors and their horses. Rangers quip about the historical monument in Coyote Canyon. People think it's a brass plaque. Nope. It's cowboy Vern Whitaker, boss of the Anza-Borrego horse camp.

Point Lobos
State Reserve

"The greatest meeting of land and water in the world." . . . "Crown Jewel" of the California park system. . . . Dante's Inferno and Paradiso conjoined. The bursting sea, the intricate folds of cove and headland, the cliff-hung cypresses, life at surf's edge— all combine to bring a shower of superlatives upon Point Lobos. Beyond Devil's Cauldron (left), Pacific breakers hammer the Sea Lion Rocks, whose residents lounge, skirmish, and bark, undeterred by any except the wildest storms. Quieter, pudgier harbor seals (lower left) frequent gentler nooks. When Point Lobos came into state hands in the 1930s, its neighbors at Carmel—the "Seacoast of Bohemia," a sort of wild life-style refuge for writers and artists—dreaded the impact of a park, with noisy mobs. Point Lobos became a state reserve, "held in trust as nature had designed it." Today, Carmel has crowds; Point Lobos has none, limiting visitors to 450 at a time.

FOLLOWING PAGES: Where have all the devils gone? Not to sheltered China Cove. Jade lapping the pocket beach invites a dip, but water temperatures, averaging 52°F year-round, discourage it.

On Monterey lowlands "the fogs are in possession," wrote Robert Louis Stevenson; "they crawl in scarves. . . ." Wraiths like those that appeared to him still haunt Point Lobos today, pallid limbs wildly askew, wearing fog like a shroud. Yet, though the Monterey cypresses bow to wind and spray, they do not flee. The species does not propagate naturally anywhere except on this headland and one a few miles north. The battle-scarred Old Veteran, in the foreground, reveals some of the tactics of survival—the leeward lean, the trunk swelling to buttress the load, the deep roots. The veteran has survived for about two centuries— not much more than middle age. Scientists estimate the life span of a Monterey cypress as 350 years.

Na Pali Coast
State Park

Traveling light pays handsome dividends on the Kalalau Trail, where the terrain and the views take the breath away. The 11-mile trail on Kauai's Na Pali coastland climbs the cliffsides and dips to sea level. Many hikers turn back at the first valley; others ease the trek with an overnight at a beach campground, where footprints on the sands linger only until the next incoming tide. Winter surf obliterates the entire beach, which milder seas restore. Spiky leaves of the hala tree have for centuries provided Hawaiians with fiber for fans, sleeping mats, sandals, baskets, and balls. Of a mother with loving children it is said: "Her children are like the many-rooted hala of the mountain side."

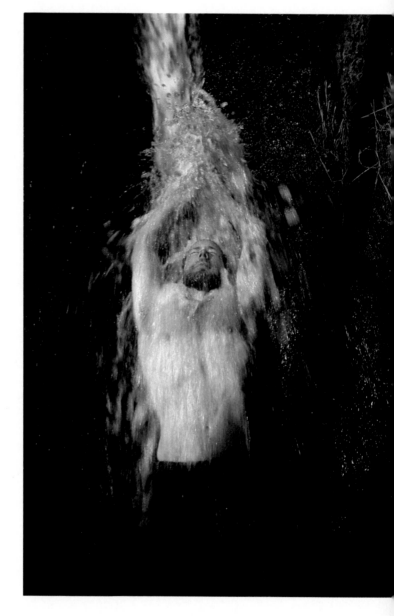

Out of a cleft in the pali,
Hanakapiai Falls spills down 400
feet—and that's only the half of it.
Above the spout, hidden from view,
the upper cataract plunges an equal
distance. Just to see the lower half,
hikers detour two miles from the
Kalalau Trail, ascending a valley
that grows ever narrower, ever
steeper, with the risk of rockfalls
and flash flooding. Soft, misty
winds play across the amphitheater;
tall kukui trees flank the outlet
stream. Hawaii honors the kukui
as the state tree, for its beauty and
ancient utility. From the trunks
the people fashioned canoes;
from the roots, black dye. Strung
together, kukui nut kernels burned
as candles; crushed, they yielded
lamp oil. The mythical little people,
the menehune, spun the nuts
as tops; and Hawaiians still joke
about the vaunted purgative powers
of the raw kernels. At Kalalau,
terminus of the 11-mile coastal trail,
a broad valley fringed with fluted
cliffs offers campsites on the beach,
in caves, or in woodland, and
an easily accessible waterfall for
refreshment (right) and socializing.

Wallowa Lake
State Park

Children of all ages play a summer game at the campground. Eastern Oregon sunshine lures vacationers from the misty coast. Wildlife, such as the golden-mantled ground squirrel below, finds campers eager to ease the struggle for survival.

FOLLOWING PAGES: *Landmarks around glacial Wallowa Lake commemorate human struggle. Flanking mountains bear the names of famed adversaries—Chief Joseph of the Nez Perce, right, and Gen. O. O. Howard. Bonneville Mountain, center, honors an explorer. Near the wintry cottonwoods rests old Chief Joseph, father of the warrior.*

NOTES ON CONTRIBUTORS

A native of Connecticut, THOMAS B. ALLEN was a member of the Society's staff from 1965 to 1981. Among other notable books, he wrote *Vanishing Wildlife of North America* and edited *The Marvels of Animal Behavior*. As a free lance, he is author of *War Games* and co-author of a biography of Adm. Hyman Rickover.

National Geographic Photographer JAMES P. BLAIR, a native of Philadelphia, graduated from the Illinois Institute of Technology and worked for a television station in Pittsburgh before he joined the Society's staff in 1965. He covered the nation's ecosystems for *Our Threatened Inheritance*, a timely report on federal lands. In 1977 he won the Overseas Press Club award for the best photographic reporting from abroad.

SEYMOUR L. FISHBEIN, a native of New York City, served as a pilot in the U. S. Navy in World War II, earned a B.A. at George Washington University, and worked for the *Washington Post* before he came to the Society in 1962. As a writer and editor, he has contributed to many books since.

A Texan by birth, DIXIE FRANKLIN grew up in Lufkin; she has kept her accent in Michigan's Upper Peninsula, her home since 1962. A free lance since 1976, she is currently president of the Midwest Travel Writers Association and vice president of the Michigan Outdoor Writers Association. Her outdoor preferences include cross-country skiing and snowshoe hikes as well as canoeing. This is her first assignment for Special Publications.

RAYMOND GEHMAN, a South Carolinian from Greenville, earned his bachelor's degree in journalism at the University of Missouri. Since 1982 he has been a staff photographer for the *Virginian-Pilot* and the *Ledger-Star* in Norfolk, winning numerous honors. As an intern at the Society in 1979, he worked on the Minneapolis-St. Paul story photographed by Annie Griffiths for NATIONAL GEOGRAPHIC; this is his first assignment for Special Publications.

Free-lance photographer ANNIE GRIFFITHS, born in Minneapolis, grew up there and earned a B.A. in photojournalism there, at the University of Minnesota. Since 1980 she has had varied assignments for the Society, and received awards from the Associated Press and the National Press Photographers' Association.

DAVID ALAN HARVEY grew up in Virginia Beach and earned his B.A. in journalism at Virginia Commonwealth University, with graduate study at the University of Missouri. A free lance since January 1987, he was a National Geographic photographer from 1978 through 1986. His assignments have taken him to Southeast Asia, Spain and Tunisia, Honduras and the Arctic. His work for Special Publications includes *America's Atlantic Isles*.

A native of Delaware, JANE R. McCAULEY went southeast to earn her B.A. at Guilford College and do graduate work at the University of North Carolina. Expert in needlecraft, she takes a particular interest in textile and fabric arts. Since 1970 she has contributed to all the products of Special Publications; she is writing her fifth book for children, *Africa's Animal Giants*.

THOMAS NEBBIA, currently a free lance, was a National Geographic photographer from 1958 to 1966, with many assignments for the Magazine. This is his first major coverage for Special Publications. A native of Rochester, New York, he began his career as a newspaper photographer in Columbia, South Carolina.

A resident of Brooklyn, MICHAEL W. ROBBINS is editor of *Oceans*. As a free lance, he wrote the 1981 Special Publication *High Country Trail: Along the Continental Divide*. He has contributed chapters to other books, and has also written for TRAVELER. His eastern affiliations include a B.A. from Colgate, an M.A. from Johns Hopkins, and a Ph.D. from George Washington University.

Breakfast of champions: The great Thoroughbred gelding Forego crops the bluegrass at his retirement home—the Kentucky Horse Park. Three times Horse of the Year, Forego won nearly two million dollars in purses before he stopped racing in 1978. The unique shrine of the sport of kings hints at the variety of our state parks—preserves of living history and culture, parks for paddlers and hikers and climbers, and vast reaches of wilderness that rival the glories of the national parks.

ACKNOWLEDGMENTS

The Special Publications Division acknowledges with pleasure the permission of Random House, Inc., to reprint excerpts from "Tor House" and "De Rerum Virtute," by Robinson Jeffers, from *Selected Poems*, © 1963 and 1965 by Donnan Jeffers and Garth Jeffers.

The Division thanks the many state officials and agencies, and other specialists, that have given generous assistance during the preparation of this book. It gratefully acknowledges the help of individuals and organizations named or quoted in the text, and of those cited here: John W. Attig, Charles Beveridge, William Chiat, William Clark, Lee Clayton, Elnore Corbett, Hellmut Doelling, Bobbie Gallup, James A. Hanson, Larry Jones, Kenneth I. Lange, Wayne Melquist, Jack McNeel, Phyllis Myers, Ray Newman, Ronald Nowak, Robert O. Petty, Gary Randorf, Richard D. Reger, Robert F. Rundle, Alfred Runte, Jerry Smith, Mike Storey, Charles Whiton, William F. Wilson; the Center for Creative Photography, University of Arizona.

Library of Congress CIP Data
America's outdoor wonders.
   Bibliography: p.
   Includes index.
   1. Parks—United States. 2. Recreation areas—United States. 3. United States—Description and travel—1981- . I. National Geographic Society (U.S.). Special Publications Division.
E160.A58   1987   917.3'04927   87-11001
ISBN 0-87044-624-X
ISBN 0-87044-629-0 (lib. bdg.)

198

ADDITIONAL READING

The reader may consult the *National Geographic Index* for related articles. The Society has published numerous books dealing with scenic and wilderness areas and with wildlife. *Our Threatened Inheritance: Natural Treasures of the United States* deals with federal lands; many of the issues discussed in it involve state policies as well.

Especially timely, and highly pertinent, is *Americans Outdoors: The Legacy, The Challenge.* This is the report of the President's Commission on Americans Outdoors, recently published by Island Press, Washington, D. C. It brings together data on outdoor resources, national, state, and local; reviews developments since 1962; and offers proposals for the future appropriate to nationwide changes in residence patterns, family structure, and employment and leisure.

The following may also be of interest: Orrin and Lorraine Bonney, *Guide to the Wyoming Mountains and Wilderness Areas;* Sherwin Carlquist, *Hawaii: A Natural History;* Champ Clark, *The Badlands;* Patricia D. Duncan, *Tallgrass Prairie;* Kenneth and Helen Durant, *The Adirondack Guide-Boat;* Alvin M. Josephy, Jr., *The Nez Perce Indians and the Opening of the Northwest;* Howard Kirschenbaum et al., *The Adirondack Guide;* Lowell and Diana Lindsay, *The Anza-Borrego Desert Region;* Charles Capen McLaughlin, ed., *The Papers of Frederick Law Olmsted;* Perry H. Merrill, *Roosevelt's Forest Army;* Richard F. Pourade, *The Explorers;* Alfred Runte, *National Parks: The American Experience;* Hilary Steward, *Cedar;* Charlton M. Tebeau, *A History of Florida;* Freeman Tilden, *The State Parks;* William Chapman White, *Adirondack Country;* Charis Wilson and Edward Weston, *California and the West.*

Composition for *America's Outdoor Wonders* by the Typographic section of National Geographic Production Services, Pre-Press Division. Printed and bound by Holladay-Tyler Printing Corp., Rockville, Md. Film preparation by Catherine Cooke Studio, Inc., New York, N.Y. Color separations by Lanman Progressive Company, Washington, D.C.; Lincoln Graphics,Inc., Cherry Hill, N.J.; and NEC, Inc., Nashville, Tenn.